The GIFT BEARER

Based on a True Event

KEN CARTER MD

The Gift Bearer
Copyright © 2020 Kenneth Carter

Interior Design by Kristine Cotterman
Exodus Design Studio

Editing by David Ferris

ISBN:

First printing: 2020
Printed in the United States of America

Unique like a shell upon the shore:

A story of a doctor and his hermit,

an exemplum of living with the self, less.

To: Richard,

Thank you for your many sermons and that sound advice to not just read but "wrestle with the Word." Every physician should walk in life with such a friend.

To: Sydney,

Thank you for the inspiration and the memory of building castles in the sand. My life would have had a void if you had not been there. Every father should dream of such a gift.

To: Patty,

Thank you for your love, your encouragement, and your testament that you share through your word and example. I fear where I would have been, and where I was going, if you had not entered my life. Every husband should yearn for such a gift.

Contents

DEFINITION: Exemplum   I

INTRODUCTION   III

PROLOGUE: Becoming Aware of the Exemplum   VII

CHAPTER 1: Salesmen Wear Blue Coats   1

CHAPTER 2: Not So Thick and Not So Thin   11

CHAPTER 3: The First Encounter   19

CHAPTER 4: The Phone Call   33

CHAPTER 5: Days of Gratitude   43

CHAPTER 6: The Body and Its Many Parts   53

CHAPTER 7: The Smells of Christmas   63

CHAPTER 8: A Time of Replenishing   71

CHAPTER 9: The Encounter of Mortality   83

CHAPTER 10: Living the Life of Self-discovery   91

CHAPTER 11: Shoes Under the Bed   99

CHAPTER 12: The Lesson of the Three-legged Stool   109

CHAPTER 13: The Laying on of Hands   123

CHAPTER 14: The Gift   131

CHAPTER 15: It's OK to Let Go   143

CHAPTER 16: Graduation Day   155

CHAPTER 17: A Broken Shell   163

CHAPTER 18: Wearing the Long White Coat   175

CHAPTER 19: A Time to Surrender   181

EPILOGUE   195

Exemplum:

A short narrative in verse or prose; a brief anecdotal story that teaches a moral lesson or point that can reinforce a doctrine of religious belief.

This genre sprang from classical, medieval, and Renaissance literature.

In Latin, the word means "example."

Introduction

It was a time when life was much simpler. It was a time when a kid could play outside all day, out of the sight of parents. There was no cell phone carried in your hip pocket. Cell phones did not exist, nor were they needed. Our parents were fearless. They were known as the greatest generation. We were called the baby boomers, and we were told that anything was possible.

It was the best of times to be a dreamer. It was the worst of times to be lazy. It was a time when a teenager who had ten dollars in his pocket could put gas in his car, take his girl on a date, and still have enough money left over to share a pizza and a soda pop after the movies.

We parked in the local Tastee-Freeze and watched the muscle cars cruising by. We did not have computers, tablets, or video games. We had pinball machines.

It was the best of times to be passionate. It was the worst of times to be bored. It was a time when not all moms had to work out of the home, and dads had time in the evening to play catch with their sons. We did not have streaming services, designer jeans, or texting. We had face to face relationships and sock hops at school. We had 4th of July parades with firetrucks and baton twirlers leading the high school band marching down Main Street. Our 45's were records, not guns.

It was a perfect time to become a doctor. It was a time when a young intern could make the diagnosis of acute appendicitis by laying hands on the belly without relying on a CT scanner to confirm his findings. We did not have AIDS or an opioid crisis. We did not have MERSA and other antibiotic-resistant bacterium. Penicillin seemed a panacea. We did not have hospitalists who treated us in the hospital. We had caring family doctors who knew our names and family and who would make a house call if needed.

Freedom rang out loudly.

Optimism sounded out clearly.

Opportunity jumped out boldly.

Passion leaped out lively.

I was that baby boomer.

I was that dreamer.

I was that teenager.

I was the one marching down Main Street.

I was that person who wanted to make house calls.

My story is a brief anecdotal account of my medical school days. Does it teach a moral point that can reinforce a religious belief? Is this story exemplary? It may not have sprung from classical or medieval times, but it was in the past!

The stories that "make the physician" are truthful. The events that led to my acceptance and selected subsequent events during medical school did take place. Perhaps they were embellished slightly in the passing of time. However, they had resounding effects upon me. I admittedly lack the imagination to have fabricated them. To have lived these stories was amazing.

There once was a hermit who lived on a barrier island on the Atlantic shore. I knew people who had met him but never had the opportunity myself. I can only imagine what he was like. Oh, if he could have had the life that I have created! Oh, if he had been able to influence others that crossed his path!

The gift of the hermit is also real. All his thoughts once lived, swirling around in my mind. To unravel his wisdom has taken me a lifetime and years to put down on paper. Those thoughts are now revealed in the life of the hermit. His gift is timeless. May it be full of hope and peace to all.

Now, let me take you back to a simpler time.

PROLOGUE

Becoming Aware of the Exemplum

It can take a lifetime to become aware of a pivotal moment in time. And so it is now, as I find myself sitting in a beach chair inches from the water's edge. I am looking directly at the ocean. The cloudless sky with its fiery sun and burning rays of transparent energy cause the curl of each wave to sparkle just below the perfectly flat, blue horizon. As far as the eye can see, the ocean and its beauty seem endless. Not a single object breaks this panoramic view. Methodically with my feet, I begin to dig a deeper and deeper hole in the moist sand. A small tidal pond slowly fills with salty water. The water from the pool cools my sandy, suntanned feet. I notice that thousands, maybe millions of tiny broken pieces of shell lie randomly scattered above the slowly advancing water's edge both in the hole and along the entire shoreline. This collage of mollusk shells is a remnant of many previously living creatures. I imagine it represents a bone yard. Each shell is unique, adding beautiful color and artistic detail to this otherwise barren shoreline.

A pelican flies just above the ocean's glistening surface. Suddenly and effortlessly it dives into the ocean and partakes of his midday snack. I can even see his gullet rhythmically contract with peristaltic waves as he swallows his catch of the day. Most assuredly, this pelican is taking as much pleasure in eating this fish as I am being the observer of the feast. My downy, feathered friend settles down and rides the waves, bobbing up and down, much like a small piece of cork in a glass of wine. This carefree fellow must live a wonderful life, I imagine. There he sits with his belly full of fish, knowing the abundance of the ocean. He spends his day flying, diving, eating, and bobbing in the waves. He worries about nothing. He spends his evenings on a cozy nest atop a mudflat on the bay side of the island. He lives his days knowing that the next day will be as free, abundant, and blissful as the day before. Oh, to have his wings and soar like him; what a life it would be.

Meanwhile, a fiddler crab, a few feet away from my chair, frantically kicks out minuscule pebbles of sand from his burrow. Just as quickly, he scurries sideways into his oceanfront home. With the discipline of a skilled mason, every minute or so, this proudly domestic creature repeats his act of labor and fortifies his home in the sand. I close my eyes and imagine what this creature's life is like in that cool, moist, dark hole in the sand. When he comes out and makes an accounting of his surroundings, he suddenly bolts away and stops as if in fear. He scouts point to point and, with his eyes moving from side to side, looks for nearby danger. If he suspects the least amount of a threat, he dashes with lightning speed directly into his hole of security. I imagine that he must live his life in constant fear and moments of sheer panic. His life is such a contrast to his neighbor the pelican several hundred feet away floating on the ocean's surface.

I lean back, resting my head on the back of my chair. I tilt the brow of my baseball cap, the sun warms my face, and I slowly close my sleepy eyes. For a moment, the calmness of the day overtakes me. I stop digging the hole with my feet, and my mind starts to fade. I am awakened by the sound of a hose splashing water on the side of a house. A frustrated elderly lady is struggling to clean the salty film from her condominium's oceanfront sliding glass door. She appears fragile; however, she is obsessed by the chore at hand and works desperately to obtain the perfect view from her living room. I imagine that she must treat her home as an aquarium and she is quite comfortable living inside and looking out at the world around her. As I continue to watch this ritual of labor, I can only conclude that the little lady lives alone, may have become fearful of the outside world, and takes pride knowing that her perfectly clean aquarium can protect her from a world full of predators.

Further down the beach, two teenagers, hand in hand, run and jump into the breaking waves. They scream with pleasure as a large wave breaks over them, and they come up for air. They begin to shiver from the shock of the contrasting coolness of ocean water on their burning, suntanned bodies. They gaze into each other's eyes with excitement and wonder. They think they are alone in this moment. They appear to say to the world that everything is in order here, their life is carefree, and nothing else matters in the universe. It is as if the coolness of the ocean's spray has frozen them in time. I imagine that someday in the future, the two of them will make a commitment to each other, and they will begin to share their lives together. My mind wanders, and I begin to fear that they will not find the secret that bonds two people as soul mates for a lifetime. There is a part of me that wants to run to them and share the secret: that the true joy in life comes from the daily desire to completely give of yourself to another, without asking for anything in return. Simply, it is the gift of your complete self, given freely. I refrain, and their moment of bliss goes on uninterrupted. In my heart, I hope for the best for the two of them.

I look down the beach to my right, and there sits a father with his eight-year-old daughter who is making a sandcastle by dropping wet sand from her hands. A concoction of sunscreen oil and sand covers her legs, and the sun has bleached her long blonde hair as light as the sand itself. She straddles the bucket full of water and sand. She dips her hand in for another layer of sand for the towering make-believe castle. She speaks to her dad about the beautiful princess that lives in the mighty castle. The dad playfully crawls on hand and knee to build a wall around the fortified kingdom and adds to the romantic story by describing the handsome prince who will soon arrive to greet the awaiting princess. As the castle grows, so does the story of the people who live out their lives in this fantasy kingdom. The girl and her dad play together as if this day will last forever.

I imagine them growing older. The play of building sandcastles will one day turn into moving furniture into an apartment at college. She still has her long hair, but now she discretely applies a little makeup and mascara to accent her sky blue eyes. She will speak to her dad about a handsome young man she has met. The father may add to the story by suggesting that she should invite him over to her new apartment and cook him dinner one evening. The dad reflects for a moment and thinks of lessons he has learned in his life. He seizes the moment and suggests to his daughter that the real and lasting value in life is in the relationships you nurture, not the material things accumulated from a life of abundance. Again, the two are unaware that this precious time is passing so quickly, and they continue to work together painting the walls of her room and arranging furniture.

I gaze at the horizon of sea and sky and discover that my pelican friend has left his afternoon cafe and flown away. I look for my bug-eyed crawling beach partner, the crab, and as I expect, he has settled down into his home for a well-deserved afternoon nap. I turn around, and the old lady is sitting on her porch, looking back at her aquarium, and drinking an iced tea. She appears to be worshipping her aquarium, thankful that at least for a day her window is free of salty deposits. As if a story is unfolding, the two teenagers to my left have retired to their blanket. The boy reaches into his ice chest and shares a cola with his girl to quench their thirst. They appear quite satisfied with each other. The tide is now coming in, and the sandcastle is taking a beating from the waves. The father and daughter have gathered their beach towels and toys, and they now run to the shoreline. The father attempts to wash the sand from his daughter's almost totally covered body. Several feet into the sea, small waves break over her, and the sand returns to its permanent home on the ocean floor. He carries his tired little girl in his arms to their cottage that lies just over the rolling sand dunes. As they leave, the setting sun starts to cast long shadows down the beach.

The incoming tide has finally reached the canopy of broken seashells along the shore. These shells have tumbled like this for years in the sand as salty water ripples over them. A tinkling sound can be heard as thousands of broken pieces of shell hit against each other and break the silence of the day. I imagine that this musical sound, a sound much like the cymbals in an orchestra, has occurred day after day, forever. Slowly time moves on, and slowly the shells erode, break into smaller and smaller pieces, and eventually return to the shore as sand.

The sun is burning my shoulders, and it's starting to hurt. I smell the salt in the air as the afternoon wanes. Suddenly I am startled. For the first time today, I hear the waves breaking as they march into the shoreline. They have been crashing like this all day long, but I have not heard them. Intently I home in on the rhythmic beating of the ocean's song, and I come to the realization that the beat of these waves has been playing like this forever. The sound of its fury was there when I was a little kid playing at the beach with my parents. The sound of the waves was there when I was a teenager riding my boogie board for hours at a time. This eternal, endless chain of waves striking this shore has been here for centuries. Today I have witnessed only a brief moment in the life of this seashore. And all of this is but a blink of a creator's eye in the eternal life of this inspiring place. I have sat here today and touched the salty ocean with my feet, watched the waves rhythmically break along the shore, and heard the gentle rush of wind blow past my ear. Despite the constant ebb and flux of the tides and the ever-changing winds, this scene in other ways has never really changed with the passing of time. It is as if the ocean, the tides, and the shore have an identity of their own and continue to play out their lives independent to my own.

Today I am only an observer.

But I see my footsteps here in the sand.

And, here is the hole that I dug with my feet

Perhaps having been here this day in this moment, I have made a difference in this everlasting, beautiful place. For the brief time that our two lives crossed we were dependent upon each other, and we each made an impression upon one another. Does this make sense to anyone but me? Would it be easier to comprehend if one knew that nothing in this world happens by chance and that everything occurs for a reason? Is there a purpose in living? Must everything be in harmony? Perhaps I was destined to cross paths with this place and be united.

Now, having come to this catharsis for the first time, I have become aware of the sea, the waves, and the shoreline. I see the inherent order here. Perhaps in the past, the confusion of my thinking mind, trying to analyze and rationalize the beauty of this heavenly place made me miss its hidden harmony. There is sacredness here that suggests a higher order in everything. Has this place been perfected by a loving creator so that I can now become a conscious participant? How joyful life becomes when one is still and alert. Becoming realigned with this awesome display of nature and its totality of life gives me a sense of calm and a peace of mind.

I believe I have come to deeply appreciate the sea, and I have become part of this endless beauty. It is as if I belong to the sea and the sea belongs to me. Perfectly placed, just like the colorful display of broken shells along the shoreline, we have always been, are presently, and forever will be joined. Is this the way it has been scripted? Could it be any other way than what it is? Is it my purpose to play my part, perfectly choreographed, in the endless story written by a higher order? Perhaps, there is a heavenly kingdom among me. And today at this pristine moment in time, I have become aware and become a part of it. As I come to the realization, my mind retraces the path that lead me to this point.

Everyone has a story to tell. Each person's story is full of dreams, fears, and the consequences of each. This story begins at one of those pivotal moments in life when an event and the course it follows indelibly impact your life. Such an extraordinary moment can be like the stone thrown in the pond. When, at the exact second it hits the water, it creates ripples that can traverse the entirety of the pond. These ripples immediately change the appearance of the surface of the pond. Often the stone is small and subsequently produces only a small shift. The pivotal moment in my young life when I choose to start my story, the stone if you will, is instead quite large. This rock thrown in my pond made huge ripples in my life. The outcome not only affected me but also the many people I would come into contact with. My story begins when I was 21 years old. Once the stone is thrown and the ripples begin, it suddenly turned audacious!

CHAPTER 1

Salesmen Wear Blue Coats

I am not accustomed to sitting on hard granite steps, which were likely cut from an open-faced quarry on the side of a North Carolina mountain many years ago and placed here to withstand the weather and the passage of time. These perfectly sculptured steps are just now losing their coolness from the early morning air and most assuredly in an hour or so the rising August sun will make them warm to the touch.

I sit upon these steps wearing my best Sunday attire. I have worn these wing-tipped shoes more than usual these past six months. All the interviews and formal events surrounding my graduation from college have given them a good work out lately.

The journey that led me to these gray stone steps was full of pure joy and heart-breaking setbacks. Having been the first to earn a degree (magna cum laude no less) made my parents quite proud. Without question, college was a time of growth. It was also a time of anticipation. That period was the most extraordinary event of my early life. I was excited, committed, and ready for anything life would throw at me. I was ready to enter medical school and become a doctor.

But then came seven rejection letters. They say that you can feel the thickness of the letter and determine the outcome of your application. Thick is good! Thin means, "We regret to inform you." For the past three months all I have known is thin.

Big questions loom over me. What to do in life? What if I don't get in? Has all that disciplined study in college been in vain?

An hour ago, I entered the office of admissions to a prestigious medical school, my last remaining hope. I walked up those granite steps and introduced myself to Miss Simpson, the secretary to the dean of admissions. She was a soft-spoken young woman in her twenties who appeared capable of handling any discerning request. Professional in appearance and demure, she seemed like the kind of girl you take back home and introduce to your parents.

She asked, "Do you have an appointment with the dean?"

Her smile faded quickly when I said, "I do not have an appointment. I am on the waiting list for admissions. I just need to speak to the dean if I could."

She appeared unphased. She had probably been inundated with similar requests all summer long. She attempted another smile and reluctantly said that the dean was quite busy this time of the year. However, if I was willing to wait for Dr. Johnston to return, perhaps he may be able to add me in somewhere late in the day. I told Miss Simpson that I would wait outside and return around 3:00 pm.

I thought to myself as I walked out of the office, "I bet she thinks that I will not return, but oh, I will be back!"

I found a secluded area in the atrium and sat down upon the those hot granite steps. There I patiently remained, sitting and waiting for the outcome of the day.

Time seems to move slower when you are worrying about the immediate future. What if the dean does not return to his office today? I should have called beforehand and scheduled a time for an appointment! What if he agrees to see me and I don't come across as confident? What if he thinks that I have been inappropriate to just show up at his office and ask if there is any change in my status? What if this August sun starts to make me sweat and I look ragged and drained when I meet him?

OK, so here comes another attack of the "what-if's." There is no real threat here. The sky is not falling. But all these thoughts make this waiting worse than it is. I take off my coat and take a deep breath. I begin to observe my surroundings and somehow my mind stops racing and the anxious thoughts leave.

The entrance into the hospital becomes busy with several groups of individuals in white coats. Some of them are older and wear long white coats; some are my age, wearing a shorter version of the lab coat. I suppose each to be a doctor of varying rank and order. Many sport a stethoscope in a side pocket. The younger doctors have filled their pockets with note cards and several small books stuffed with papers that make the pockets bulge. Each doctor appears confident and has his name elegantly embroidered on the chest of his coat. Each identity is completed by a hospital tag with picture ID. I think to myself; they do not know how lucky they are to have that exclusive access.

Occasionally, a doctor entering the hospital will glance down and acknowledge me. They all appear tired, especially the younger doctors. I attempt to make eye contact with them and smile politely; however, their expressions never really change. Mostly they just avoid me, never speaking, and briskly continue on. I wonder if they know what I am doing here. They do not even see me!

My attire appears quite different than the passing doctors. My khaki pants, white shirt, wing-tipped shoes, and blue sport jacket are appropriate for my present destination. Perhaps, they assume that I am a traveling salesman trying to sell my wares. I do look the part! Without question, they are not that far off in their thinking. Humility is one of the most noble of virtues. Somewhere, I have heard that humility comes before honor. These many young doctors walk by seemingly full of honor. I certainly feel more humility than honor. It sure is hard to feel any honor when you are sitting on these steps and sweating. It is difficult to imagine ever having a white coat to wear, being able to freely walk through these doors, or even having your own stethoscope in your pocket.

Yes, looking up from this vantage point, a stethoscope in a pocket is the symbol of honor!

Finally, 3:00 pm arrived, and I returned to the dean's office. I checked in with Miss Simpson and sat in one of the leather chairs to continue my wait. Several white-coated doctors came and went. I pretended to stay busy by looking at papers in my briefcase.

Slightly startled, I jumped as I notice Miss Simpson standing in front of me. She said, "I am sorry you had to wait all day, but I have placed your application on Dean Johnston's desk. He has his last appointment at 4:00 pm. I told him that you have been patiently waiting for any opening that he may have this afternoon. I saw you sitting outside on those granite steps in the hot sun all day. Can I get you anything to drink?"

It had been a long day. It was comforting to see Miss Simpson's gentle smile and have someone acknowledge my presence. I thanked her for her kindness.

I said, "I am doing okay, but a glass of water would be nice."

She left and returned promptly with a large glass of cold water and added, "Here are some chocolate chip cookies that I made last evening. You look like you need some nourishment."

She resumed working quietly at her desk. An hour passed. Miss Simpson was a consummate professional, friendly to everyone who entered the office. She had been kind to me, as well. If being considerate, especially to the stranger, and going the extra mile to assist one in need are characteristics of hospitality, then

Miss Simpson receives the award for excellence.

It was getting late in the afternoon when I noticed she was staring at me but no longer smiling. She appeared to have connected with my emotions. She seemed to understand my frustration but also seemed aware of my concerns and even my doubts. Her eyes that once had that sparkle of joy now looked sad. Not wanting her to feel sorry for me, I looked away.

The hour passed slowly in that office. I glanced up and noticed Miss Simpson checking her watch. It was past four o'clock. She stood up and took a deep breath, as if to gather courage. With a determined look on her face, she walked into the dean's office and shut the door.

Several minutes later she returned and announced with satisfaction, "Dean Johnston will now see you."

I stood up from my chair and thought, "What just happenned in that office? I hope I don't blow this opportunity!"

I squared my shoulders and walked to the door of his office. I sighed and said to myself, "I just caught the pass, and it's my opportunity to make the winning touchdown."

As I entered the room, he stood up from behind his desk and said, "I am Richard Johnston, Dean of Admissions. I understand that you have been here all day waiting to speak to me. I have reviewed your application and understand that you are on the waiting list. Have a seat and tell me a little about yourself." The late afternoon rays of sunlight fell slanting throught the window. He sat down in one of the two leather chairs placed comfortably in front of his large wooden desk. I had just sat down across from him when he broke the silence of his office. "You do understand that there are only two weeks before the freshman students begin their year? Charles, by being placed on the waiting list, we have determined that you are well qualified and honestly just as capable as any of the 76 young men and women who have already been given a position. We also recognize that there are hundreds of applicants who did not make the list that would make excellent physicians. Unfortunitity, there are only 76 positions available in the freshman class each year." His voice became subdued but he continued to speak with conviction. "I understand that it is difficult to be on the waiting list for admissions. At this point, it is extremely unlikely that a position will become available."

It was then that I looked directly into his eyes and said, "Something inside me told me that I had to come speak to you today. My heart is telling me that I need to do everything possible and explain to you the reason why this school should accept me for admission."

For the next twenty minutes, I did most of the talking. The dean seemed to be listening intently and occasionally asked a question about my intentions.

I took solace in the six-hour drive back home that evening. It had been an emotionally exhausting day. I tried to replay the words we exchanged during the meeting, but the memory of what occurred in our brief encounter seemed lost already. I do remember leaving the office and seeing Miss Simpson smiling brightly.

As I passed her desk, she politely said, "Hang in there, Charles Carpenter."

I recall wanting to say something of remembrance, much like the final passage of a play, but the only spontaneous thought that came to my mind was, "I appreciated your smile today. Thank you."

I walked out of the office, thinking, "I should have told her that chocolate chip cookies are my favorite, and I should have at least thanked her for them!" But, I never have been quick with words or wit when it comes to responding to young ladies. I will never know just what she had said to the dean, but I believe that she went the extra mile for me. Her words were resposible for opening the door to his office. I will never forget what she did for me.

I stopped on the granite steps as I was leaving. Several doctors again passed wearing their white coats. I thought to myself that it was okay for me to wear a blue coat and sell myself. I just needed the opportunity to speak to the one who had the power to make the final decision. Maybe I received a little stroke of luck or grace that day, call it what you will. With a timely and simple act of kindness from an empathetic secretary, I was granted that opportunity.

Yes, I was the salesman today, trying to sell myself to another who held all the cards. In college, I was told of a famous legal case in which a judge handed down a decision that said, "There is never any harm in asking." What if my asking had made a difference in my application? If I had only graduated from a large, elite university. Would name recognition make a difference in the selection process? The college that I attented was known for its small classes and great teaching at a more personal level. At least the dean had seen my application again and could put a face to it. He had the awesome responsibility to say "yes" or "no." By signing his name to a letter, he could determine a person's destiny. He could set one's path in life in an entirely different direction.

This authority, that the Dean of Admissions has over the applicants, does not seem fair, especially when you are the one sitting in the hot sun. One can only hope that the man with authority will use the power seriously and make wise decisions.

All I can do next was pray that the traveling salesman, wearing his blue coat, did his job well today.

The day had been a struggle. The summer sun was brutal. Time moved slowly. I may have made no difference in my application. At least if all else fails, I received some delicious chocolate chip cookies out of the ordeal.

Two days passed after I met with Dr. Johnston. I wondered if my application was on his desk or if it had been filed away in one of the many cabinets in his office. I was back to the usual routine of getting up early, eating breakfast, and waiting for the mailman to arrive. Again, I walked to the mailbox, hoping that a thick letter would arrive and make this a special day. I steeled myself against the idea of checking the mail. I had become somewhat accustomed to rejection and benign neglect. After all, I had completed this ritual almost every day for the past three months. Without any emotion or anticipation, I approached the mailbox and opened it.

I noticed a letter addressed to me. It was not so thin! It was from the last remaining medical school, the one that I had just visited.

The letter seemed thicker than all the others. Could it be the one, the one letter that I had been dreaming about for so long?

I held it in my hand.

It was not thin

CHAPTER 2

Not So Thick and Not So Thin

What could it be? This letter was not thin like the others nor was it exceptionally thick. What could this mean?

With my heart pounding in my chest, I took a deep breath and opened the letter. How nice, I have been added to the newsletter mailing list for the medical school. I imagine that Dean Johnston added my name to the mass mailing after our meeting, having no other news to share with me.

I grabbed a Coke from the refrigerator and began to read the front-page article. The headline said, "Medical school receives all time high number of candidates for admissions." I read on, "This year 2005 candidates apply for the 76 positions available for the freshman class beginning in 2 weeks."

I thought to myself, how cruel. I finally received a thick letter from a medical school, and all it did was remind me that my chance for a seat in the class was next to impossible. The dean had told me that only two hundred applicants were placed on the waiting list initially and only about twenty of them were ever given a position in his freshman class. Positions only opened up when students who had been accepted by two schools chose a different medical school to attend. These positions filled within six weeks back in the late spring. Since then, only one applicant had been granted a position from the waiting list. He assured me that this system worked well over the many years he had been dean of admissions. He did say that in the past, occasionally, "strange things" happen around the week prior to the start of the first semester. He also said that most of the students in the freshman class had already moved to town and settled into their new homes. Despite these disturbing numbers, he reminded me that I should feel honored to have gotten this close. I wanted to remind him that this was not a game of horseshoes. In the game of getting accepted into medical school, "being close" meant nothing! I acknowledged his remarks with a subtle smile and acted as if there was some comfort in his words.

The time was drawing near. I had to make alternative plans regarding my future. Up to this point, I had not accepted the fact that attending medical school was no longer an option. For four long years I had kept the ultimate goal in front of me. Using positive reinforcement, delaying gratification, and working hard had always yielded success in the past. The game was about to change quickly, and the rules were unclear. Honestly, I did not want to make any decisions. I just wanted to be alone.

It was later that morning that my parents suggested we take the camping trailer to the beach and spend the next week relaxing in the sun. They hoped a change in scenery would lift my spirits. Since it would be unlikely that I would hear anything further from any of the schools, I agreed to the end of summer family get away. Likely, the beach would help me clear my thoughts. Sitting at the shore and making holes in the sand with my feet had given me comfort in the past. At this moment, I only needed to come up with a plan for what I was going to do for the rest of my life!

We packed the camper the next morning, and the remainder of the day we spent driving to the shore. Everyone seemed subdued that afternoon while traveling to the beach. Casual talk centered around the weather with the hot and dry summer being difficult on local farmers.

My father said, "Look at those soybeans in that field, they are all brown and dried up. That farmer should have spent some money on irrigation and saved his crop. Sometimes, you must spend money to make money! You reap what you sow."

Weather and farmers were always safe topics when my father found it difficult to communicate. The words "medical school" or "future plans" never came up in our travels that day.

We arrived late in the afternoon. I helped to set up the camping site. It was a universal ritual among campers to first unpack the "essentials" for a traditional beach experience. The shade tent was placed over the center of the picnic table. The red and white vinyl tablecloth was pinned onto the table to prevent it from blowing away. The pot of clean water was placed on the table so as to readily wash one's hands. And, of course, the plastic dish pan was set at the door of the camper to remove all the sand from your feet before entering the trailer.

Once everything was in order, I told my mom and dad that I was going to take a walk on the beach. I can always tell when my parents worry about me because each one will come up with something special, like a family tradition. We would relive happy moments from the past and avoid any discussion about any stressful matters. On this occasion, my Mom said, "I'll make your favorite for dinner tonight: lima bean soup with flat dumplings, fried chicken, and corn on the cob."

There were three of my all-time culinary favorites planned for this meal. It was obvious that she was really concerned about me.

Likewise, when my dad chimed in, "I'll get the crab pots cleaned up and go buy the chicken necks, so we can go crabbing this evening," then I knew he was similarly worried.

To both I said, "Good idea," and headed to the beach.

The beach had a rotten smell. It is not uncommon in the middle of August to find jellyfish washed up in the flotsam along the shore. Portuguese Man o' War by the hundreds were turned upside down and came to find their resting place along the beach. Similarly, dead horseshoe crabs were flipped on their backs, beginning to rot, and were filling the air with that familiar, nauseating smell of late summer. This drew the flies, congregating in mass, as well. As I walk along the beach, I noticed several seagulls lying dead at the water's edge with their decaying bodies contorted and partially obscured along the salt hay and sea whip. About a mile down the beach, I had seen four such dead gulls. I thought, "The autumn sun surely seems to be casting its deathly shadows upon many beach critters today. This beach is full of despair and gloom." Constantly looking down to avoid treading upon another carcass, I thought, "This is definitely not helping my already depressed state of mind."

I tried to think instead about the delicious food and the fun that awaited me upon return to the camping site. I imagined my mother flattening her homemade dumplings for the soup. I pictured my father tying the chicken necks into the crab cages. Both thoughts brought momentary joy to the heart.

My thoughts wandered as I looked in the distance ahead of me and realized that I would soon reach the sandy point of the island where the island continually enlarged. Rapid, perpendicular currents pushed the sand down the shore to form this area. The locals called this point "the spit." I was told as a youngster growing up around the beach that one could not swim here because the tidal currents could be very strong. We were warned to never enter the water here. There was no purpose to come this far down the island. Even fish tended to avoid swimming here. Fishing was better at the head of the island where larger fish came in to shallow water to feed. As a result, the spit was usually deserted. It was the perfect place to think about one's future.

I continued to walk past the point and gradually the newly

deposited sand started to darken in color. The smell in the air changed from the salty, deathly odor to a pungent smell. It reminded me of air pollution you find in large cities. This was the first warning that you were about to enter the salt marshes. This was the area on the backside of the island that turned from sand to mud. No one in their right mind ever walked the shoreline here. My feet started to make a sucking sound as the mud got darker and deeper. I remembered from biology classes that the brackish slurry, called detritus, was a combination of decomposing cord grass and animal matter in a solution of algae and bacteria. It's nature's nourishing soup, an energy source for the hundreds of thousands of different species that began their lives here. All life flourished here. Amazingly, all I saw and smelled was mud, which was now above my ankles.

I stopped in my tracks and considered my present dilemma. "I'm on the back side of the island somewhere in the middle between the head of the island and the spit. No one else has any reason to dwell or even wander anywhere near in this area," I thought.

Since it was a path rarely taken, I chose to continue along in the mud. As I walked, I forgot the many wandering thoughts that had troubled me when I started the jouney. I hoped to find an area where I could turn into the maritime forest, meander along a path to the sand dunes, and eventually reach the well-known other side of the island, that of the beach and the ocean. Eventually, I discovered a slightly higher, less mucky ground. I thought to myself, "It was wise to wear an old pair of sneakers today. These shoes are surely ruined, now that they are completely saturated with mud." I found a small area of marsh grass, sat for a moment, and attempted to clean the mud from my feet. I noticed a small trail that led into the maritime forest. I imagined the path to be trodden down by white-tailed deer and raccoon that wander about the island at night.

I decided to take the trail and return home to the trailer and my mom's culinary delights. "Maybe if I'm lucky, I might find a way across the island and save myself the walk through the mud again." The cord grass was thicker and higher now. This was the transition from intertidal zone to supratidal zone where the mud gives way to sand. As I reached the maritime forest, the cord grass blended into yucca plants, bayberry, and yaupon shrubs. The brush became thick like a barrier. It seemed impenetrable. I noticed another deer trail from a small break that lead into the wall of shrubs. I meandered a short distance into a tight tangle of plant life and eventually reached an even denser, foreboding wall of majestic evergreens and live oak trees. The oaks with their weathered trunks and twisting branches were well adapted to the harsh beach environment. Their waxy leaves protect them from the constant cutting of blowing sand that whipped across them. These leaves provide a protective canopy that nearly blocked out the sun. The path narrowed but seemed to lead to a definite opening among the densely vegetated area.

I continued to follow as it twisted and turned among the thicket. It was obvious that I was going deeper and deeper into the maritime forest. I stopped to consider my options. I had likely walked for a half a mile into the forest, and the trail did become more defined. Deeper and deeper into the unknown I continued. I decided to continue on the present course since turning back would again require walking through the mud and covering the whole length of the island. Besides, this intriguing path seemed to be luring me to its journey's end.

Unexpectedly, the canopy of trees opened up, and some rays of sunlight touched my face. I imagined that the breaking waves of the ocean were just a few hundred feet away, lying straight ahead. Slowly, I continued into the woods, crested an elevated sand dune, and walked down the other side into another swale. The oak tree canopy was much closer now, and there appeared to be an opening at the bottom of this swale. I traversed about ten feet. Suddenly, I stop! Ahead there was a dramatic change in the environment. The oaks had completely given way to an opening with the sun shining on clear crystals of sand. The sand was completely free of grass and debris as if someone had expended considerable effort to maintain this pristine and tranquil area. The sun was shining even brighter now on my face. I listened for the faint, rhythmic sounds of the ocean's waves in the distance. I heard nothing, only sounds of the many birds, which added to the peaceful and majestic quality of this place. I thought, "This is not natural. Nature would never produce this. It's perfectly manicured and flattened without any growth. There are swales of sand on all sides. What could this place be? Why would someone work so hard to create this place?" Then my thoughts moved on, "Do I need to make a quick retreat?" I looked around for any clues and whispered to myself, "Am I in danger?"

CHAPTER 3
The First Encounter

The sand was perfectly clear of debris, appearing as smooth as if it were raked. The clearing was about the size of a racquetball court and formed an almost perfect rectangle. All around the borders of the opening lay a massive, thick wall of brush, intertwined branches of the densely populated oak trees and thistles. The underbrush of yucca plants and bayberry bushes had been removed, and the trunks and strong branches of the oaks were well manicured. It made for an idyllic setting. The opposing sides of the swale were very steep and would prove difficult to climb. I saw a dwelling embedded in the middle of the opposing wall of sand. I froze in my tracks. I could feel the hair on the back of my neck and arms stiffen. Wide-eyed and alert, I cautiously surveyed the opening, knowing it was quite likely that someone had spent considerable effort to hide this place from intruders.

It was clear to me that this was someone's home. The dwelling was made of reinforced bags of sand that stood about eight feet high. The front of this hideaway created a perfect half circle. One could tell it extended deep into the side of the sand dune's bank. A foreboding large, heavy door stood in the center; it appeared to have weathered many storms. The sand on the dune sparkled as the setting sun cast its golden shadow upon it. The metal door was firmly closed.

I suddenly remembered a childhood story and recognized the dwelling for what it was, an old military pillbox. My father had told me that this island had served as a military reserve. During World War II, several towers were erected and manned by military spotters who were assigned to look for German U-boats off the Atlantic coast. Several of these towers remain today. There was even a museum at the other end of the island attesting to the story I had heard many years before. Many of the towers in the interior of the island had since fallen and been destroyed with the passage of time. Each observation tower was accompanied by two pillbox structures made of sandbags embedded deep into the side of the dunes. One of these structures was used for the storage of ammunition; the other larger one served as living quarters for a four-man platoon.

There was no road that serviced the island back then, so access to these towers was difficult. Each platoon would stay for two weeks and then be replaced with another team. I was excited that I had stumbled upon a World War II pillbox, and then I thought, "This place is so well groomed, there must be someone using this old war relic as their home. But who... and why?"

Then from behind me, I heard a gravelly voice say, "Good afternoon, my friend. What brings you to my home?"

I nearly jumped out of my skin, as the sound startled me. I turned around, and standing at one side of the clearing was a man of short stature with a full white beard. He had very dark eyes deeply recessed into his face. The man was staring directly at me.

My words falling over each other, I spluttered, "I am sorry that I intruded upon you. I was trying to get to the ocean side of the island, and I stumbled upon your living quarters. I guess this is your home. I am so sorry to barge in on you like this. Oh, by the way, yes, I am friendly."

He then replied, "So, you must be. Only friends come to visit by way of the back door. One can imagine since the sun is setting and the day is getting late, that perhaps you are lost, and you probably stumbled into this place accidentally." A smile crossed his face as he walked down onto the glistening sand in front of his secluded beach dwelling.

He appeared to be in his 60s, but his wrinkled, dark skin made him appear older.

He observed, "You were making a lot of noise when you were walking along the mud flats and easy to detect when you turned into the forest. Having followed you through the marsh and high scrubs, one could calculate that you may run into this place. One could tell by the way that you stopped and looked around that you were likely lost. And since you have never been here before, one can only imagine that you come in friendship. So, welcome to this home."

His demeanor was kind and innocuous. I started to calm down a bit. I imagined that he did not receive many visitors.

"With such a long walk, most people turn back before reaching this home," the bearded man said and added, "The back entrance is the longest route to this place. There are paths to the north and south that go through the maritime forest that are shorter, but rarely does anyone find their way here through the woods. The front entrance runs east and goes directly to the ocean." Then he giggled and said, "That door is kept locked. Unless someone knew where this door was located, they would get lost in the maze of sand dunes and never find their way here." He then slung the sack off his shoulder, landing it just in front of the thick metal door.

"Yes, I did enter from back here," I said pointing behind me, "the path from the west, and I can leave, if you wish. I don't mean to be a bother."

I started to turn to leave. He took off his hand-woven, cord grass, floppy brim hat and said, "There is no need for you to run off just yet. Besides, it would be rude not to sit and have something to eat before you depart."

He reached behind a tree for a small bucket. Then, he opened the sack that had been on his back, and 20 or 30 small oysters clattered into the bucket. In the shade, just beside his sandbag dwelling stood two stumps from an old oak tree. He sat down on one and gestured that I sit on the other. Immediately, he stood up with haste and said, "As a guest today, you need a drink with your meal."

He darted to the huge metal door and entered his home. He returned carrying an old milk jug half full of an orange-yellow drink and two old water bottles. He poured me a bottle of the liquid, and he began to eat the raw oysters from his haul.

For a small man, he was quite muscular, especially his legs. I imagined that he explored the island daily, gathering food, water, and other necessities. Looking at the old water bottles, I could only imagine that they had washed up on shore many days prior. Nervously, I asked, "So, uh, what kind of juice is in the bottles?"

The old man smiled and said, "Friend, this is the sweet juice of the prickly pear bush that blossoms in the spring. Its pulp makes quite a tasty beverage. If you leave it set till the fall, then it will ferment, and drinking it then can dull the senses a bit."

He giggled once more, and I noticed his pure white teeth for the first time. I decided to try the oysters, knowing that they were fresh. Besides, I had not eaten since early in the morning. Then, as I placed my mouth to the bottle to drink the juice, I hesitated for a second, but soon discovered that the prickly pear juice was quite sweet and refreshing.

As I set the bottle down a question came to my mind, and without worrying that I may offend the old man, I asked, "Are the bucket and the bottle clean? Do you have soap here?"

He continued smiling but replied seriously, "Yes, nature provides everything one needs and does so abundantly. Soap is made from the thick roots of the Spanish bayonet, better known as the yucca plant, like the one just over there," and he pointed to a grouping of shrubs on the other side of the clearing. "The yucca plant is in the lily family, the sword-shaped leaves of the plant were used along with cord grass to weave this hat.

I couldn't think of an intelligent reply, so I just said, "OK, that's good to know," and took a few more swigs. "This is rather good; it reminds me of Mello Yello. How did you keep it so cool on a day like this?"

"Young man, what are you all about?" Politely, he smiled and added, "The correctly phrased question is, what do you do for a living?" Before I could answer him, he continued on, "Wisdom is like water, it flows in places men reject. There is a hole in the hut that goes eight feet deep. The earth, just at the water's level, keeps the temperature constant at around fifty-five degrees." He stood up again, walked toward his domicile, and as he entered said, "One should live close to the land."

In a few minutes, the door swung open and the bronze-skinned man held forth a bowl of greenery. "The specialty of the house is now being served," he announced.

It was a freshly tossed salad that would have put any seaside restaurant to shame.

I excitedly asked, "How did you come up with such a beautiful salad?"

The wise man said, "He who works the land will have abundant food, but he who chases fantasies lacks judgment. Abundance is everywhere. There is no scarcity on this island. Look around, life is ever present, and the living provide for each other. The ethic of nature is to give and take and share in the bounty. All living creatures are dependent upon each other, and your server today is just one humble part of this intertwined web of life."

We both sat and started to eat the greens. There is not much that I could add to the discussion, but in a feeble attempt to be polite, I said, "This salad tastes pretty good."

Without being boastful, merely attempting to be enlightening, the old man said, "The flower petals of the yucca are plentiful this time of year." Pointing to a different, light-colored, greenish leaves continued, "You can add washed sea lettuce, the leaves and seed pods are called sea rockets, to your salad, but in three weeks their harvesting season will be over." Even though I had no idea what he was talking about, he proceeded to share more detail about his salad, "Make sure you remove the spines from the flower stems of the bull thistle then chop them up. You know, they look like celery once you add them to your salad. The dark leaves that make up the bulk of the salad are from the dewberry plant. The dressing on top of the salad is mostly the soaked reddish fruit of the winged sumac. To spice things up a bit, a pinch of glasswort was added. You may smell the aroma of sage when you are eating." The wise man chuckled and added, "A good chef always adds sea myrtle leaves to every meal. Do you know why? If you get enough sage in your body, then the horse flies will not bite you!"

"Wow," I said, "That is helpful. I got bit by three of those mean flies as I was walking here."

"Protecting your skin from infection is important when you live outside among these many creatures. In your salad today, you were given your daily dose of saw palmetto, which protects your skin from deeper infection. This recipe is given to you so that you will be enlightened. One should accept that abundance is everywhere. On this barrier island, there are thousands of examples of nature's overabundance. Like the ruddy turnstone who arrives to the island from his arctic migration just in time that millions of mussels mature on the mudflats. Therein lays his meals for days on end." The old man chuckled again and said, "It's understandable why they return each year for the mussels. They are a delicacy when steamed." After a moment of hesitancy, he concluded, "So, you see young man, losing the self and becoming a part the chain of life, one can live abundantly free of worries."

He turned to me directly and asked, "What is your story? What has led you to this opening in the forest today?"

There was a brief silence as I gathered my thoughts. I began my story to the old man, "I just graduated from college three months ago. I worked extremely hard to get good grades. I was looking forward to this summer, but what was to be a happy time has turned into a frustrating summer." I hesitated a moment, but continued, "I have always wanted to go to medical school. I've been turned down by all the schools but one. Yesterday, the last one sent correspondence that said my chances are worse than one in a thousand that I would get accepted at this late date." With some mixture of sadness and anger in my heart, I said, "I went to the beach today because I wanted to be alone. I didn't want to see anyone. Watching someone being happy on the beach, laughing and playing at the water's edge was not what I wanted to witness. Leaving civilization behind, I walked all the way around the island, to the point, through the mud."

We sat in silence until I admitted, "Guess I'm weary of worrying all the time. There's not much in my world now that can be considered joyful. Here I am an intruder in your peaceful dwelling. You probably haven't eaten a meal with anyone in months, and you end up with a basket case like me, telling you about his problems."

The old man paused, then remarked, "More like two weeks."

We stayed there eating oysters and drinking fresh juice for an hour not saying a word, the monotonous quiet broken only by an occasional slurping that one of us made when attempting to get the last drop of juice from a half-shelled oyster.

Eventually, the old man offered, "It is easy to understand your frustration. You have much to learn from your past, and you must discover how to cope with your thoughts of the future. In doing so, you can control anxious moments during these frustrating times in your life."

He paused for a moment and asked, "Do you believe that you will someday be a doctor?"

"Well, realistically, it doesn't look like it at this point in time."

He replied harshly, "Then, you never shall!"

Softening somewhat, he continued, "Being a human, living at the sea among these plants and animals, one can learn much about what makes the human condition so unique. Watch the great herons stalk their prey for hours in the shallow water estuaries. They are not frustrated as they patiently wait for their needs to be provided. The animals that live at the shore are well-adapted. The varying species of shorebirds found here are a great example of this. The bills of the different shorebirds are unique to the way they obtain their food. The sanderlings prefer to feed on shifting sand at the water's edge, running back and forth, staying ahead of the advancing waves. They can probe the sand for flies, insect larvae, and small crustaceans. The oyster catcher prefers to dine on mussels, clams, or oysters. His bill is laterally compressed and shaped like a double-edged knife. It is uniquely adapted to pry open these shellfish. The ibis, on the other hand, feeds in the marshes and has a long, thin, curved bill that allows them to probe deep into the mudflats to reach burrowing organisms like marine worms and small crabs. The black skimmer is unique in that he is adapted to fly just above the water, open his bill, and catch small fish just below the surface of the water. His lower bill is longer than the upper so that he can accomplish this feat. Never do they live in fear that their needs or wants will not be met. In all of nature there is abundance, and all needs are met."

Smiling slightly, he continued, "Along comes the human with advanced skills. He can think, solve problems, and manipulate his environment. He, too, competes for the resources that nature provides. Man can choose, has free will. This, however, can lead to his demise. He thinks about what will make him happy, then he chooses his course of action. He becomes successful. This can be a good thing, up to a point. However, the inherent problem with choosing and acquiring your wants is that you create an identity of the self. You become separate and in competition with the rest of the world. This separation leads to disharmony with other living creatures. This isolated life, existing only with self leads to doubt, fear, and frustration. He believes that there is scarcity in the world. It is then that his path becomes a struggle.

This all started with man thinking about his choices. There is a different way. There is a way to jump off this vicious cycle of fear and pain, the pain that you are experiencing just now. For some, it can take a lifetime to learn. However, once mastered, your life can be abundant, like the life of the great heron."

The sun was setting, so the old man said abruptly, "To find your way back to your home, you must leave before it gets dark. When you return to your world, remember the abundance that all living creatures have available here." Pointing with his hands in a complete circle around his body, he exhorted, "Remember all you have heard and seen here today. Think of the many choices you have to ponder."

The old man stood up and started pacing as if to place an exclamation mark upon what he was about to say. He continued, "Choose what is most important. The key to success is finding the middle ground between your fears and your hopes. Accept what happens daily in your life, but never lose sight of that which is your most important desire. Visualize your desire as if it were on a path that you are walking toward. You must remember the past, but never stop dreaming of the future. The delicate balance of both your memories and your dreams can make you thrive in the present. Do not let your life's passion make you anxious. You must always think that each day, each step along the path is one closer to your ultimate desire. Be wise and patient like the great heron. With his two feet firmly entrenched at the water's edge, he watches the water pass by. Any sway of self-doubt or any quiver of anxiety may make the heron lose focus, and in that moment his desire, that of an evening meal, may just swim away. Remember the way of the great heron. He is patient. He is focused."

The hermit smiled widely and gestured to the north side of the opening in the brush. "Follow this path through the forest for about twenty minutes. When you first see the water of the bay, the path will run out, then turn left and follow the shoreline. The mud flats are not deep there. Walk another ten minutes or so, and you will see the causeway and bridge that run to the mainland. From there you should be able to find your way back to your home."

I thanked him for the wonderful meal we shared. Then he said to me, "A gift is in order for you to take back with you for the journey that lies ahead."

With small, quick steps, he went into his fortified dwelling buried into the side of the sand dune. Upon returning, again with haste and resolution in his step, he approached me and reached for my hand. He opened the palm of my hand. From his weathered, calloused fingers, he dropped a small, perfectly round object onto my palm. I looked intently at the gift and quickly realized that it was a yellow-white pearl. The hermit, who was now standing over me, looked straight into my eyes and said slowly, "In your world the pearl is considered a scarcity. In this place, several inches below the water on the mud flats in the shell of an oyster, they are abundant. Remember, friend, as you leave this home and enter yours that there is abundance everywhere!" With firmness in his grip, he shook my hand and pointed to the direction that would lead me back to my familiar world.

His directions to the water's edge and my way back were perfect. Our discussions had ended just in time for me to witness the sun setting over the flat horizon of a calm sea. I paused for a moment to take it all in. Oh, what a wonderful afternoon, and what a wise man I had met. For a time, my anxiety over the future vanished as I took in the wisdom of the hermit.

As I looked down the shoreline of the bay to where the hermit lived, I noticed an awesome sight. There in the shadows of the setting sun, about fifty yards away, stood a great heron. Both feet stood firmly in the mud. With his neck poised for the strike and without the movement of a muscle, he stalked. Keenly aware of his moment in time, still as a statue he stood, resolute that his evening meal would soon swim by his feet.

By the time I reached the camping trailer it was dark. A full moon cast its shadow upon the roadway. I was about to learn a truth about my parents: they practice the virtue of patience. My dad always liked to eat his evening meal at 6:00 pm. When I arrived two hours late and he said nothing, it confirmed his patience and love for me. Seeing that my mom had been stirring the lima beans and flat dumplings on the stove for at least an hour showed she cared deeply for me. She only said, "Go wash your hands," without any sign of annoyance. What a blessing, to have parents live with true patience! That evening as, we sat at the dinner table my dad said, "We had a good catch today. The crabs were the biggest we have had in years!"

What a wonderful way to end the day. I had met a wise man, and I had just eaten all my favorite foods in one meal. Parents teach patience, but they also give unconditional love at the times when you need it the most. As the evening came, we sat in reclining chairs around the bonfire and watched the moon roll across the starry evening sky.

I felt relaxed. We reminisced about past summer evenings

spent together. My parents noticed that I was more content than I had been in a long time. They must have surmised that the lima beans, flat dumplings, and fried chicken had really hit the spot.

My mom asked, "Where did you get the pearl that you are holding in your hand? Is it real?"

"Oh yes, it is real. It came out of an oyster that I ate from the island." Nothing was ever asked further regarding the pearl. I never told them about the hermit. His giving of the pearl and his visit was my gift. Some things are not meant to be shared even with those closest to you.

That night in bed, I reflected upon all the words of wisdom that the hermit had shared. I was confused about much of his counsel, but the heron standing steadfast there in the mud kept reappearing in my mind. My thoughts stayed focused on the heron. Just as I was about to fall asleep, I remember thinking, "When I face the trials of the next days, I must remember the heron!"

CHAPTER 4

The Phone Call

Like many of the late summer days on the island, the morning began with a cool nip in the air, reminding all that the humid, sticky dawns of summer were behind you. I had no real plans for the day. I would go to the beach again since autumn was growing near. Those carefree, sunny days at the beach would soon be fading memories. I thought about the old man and his wise words. I reached for a piece of paper that I had stuck in my pocket. I had written down several things from memory from my visit with the hermit. I reread the following quote,

> "No one can linger in the memories of the past,
> nor can one dream only of the future.
> It is the delicate balance of the two that makes
> the acceptance of the present so meaningful."

It can be a difficult proposition to accept the reality that you must choose your path for the rest of your life. It's worse for a college graduate who has worked hard toward a singular goal for many years. I had run a good race and finished my collegiate years well. However, in the dean's eyes, I had come up just short of the trophy that would signify my acceptance to medical school. Perhaps, if I had been lucky enough to have a relative as a physician or an alumnus of the university just call in a favor on my behalf, the outcome would have been different. Being disappointed was appropriate; being dejected and bitter were not.

Therefore, I chose to remain positive. I would remain focused: think of the past, dream of the future, and accept the present for what it is. The hermit would be proud of me. I was in control of my thoughts and they were good!

It was getting late. I jumped from the bed and dressed for the beach. As I left my room, I noticed that no one was in the trailer. On cool mornings, my mother always walked and visited other campers. My father always went to the bay and checked his crab pots. I grabbed a Pop-Tart for breakfast and walked out the door. My mother was walking toward me with six fresh tomatoes that a friend had given her and said, "Your father went to fill the truck up with gas and will be back soon. I will straighten up the camper now that you are awake. You know that in a few days we will have to return home. The Labor Day holiday is a couple of days away, and we all must go back to work. And my dear, what are you going to do today?"

It did not take much thought to respond, "I'm going to go to the beach, sit in my low-back chair, read my new book, swim a little, take a jog down the beach, and just have a lazy summer day."

"Those sounds like great choices," my mother said. "I've got to go to the grocery store. I'm fixing stuffed peppers tonight."

I kissed her on the cheek. "You know that's my favorite!"

As I started to walk to the beach, my dad drove by and pulled up beside me.

"When I get back from the beach later, I'll help you with those repairs on the trailer. Is that OK with you?" I said. He gestured that that was fine, and he continued into the driveway.

Old habits die hard. On several occasions while I wasted the day relaxing on the beach, I would drift back to the dream of being in medical school, but soon realized that it would likely never become a reality. Then, I took the pearl out of my pocket and looked at it. I remembered what the hermit had said about the acceptance of the present for what it was. He said that one does not have to give up hope, and one can choose to live without fear and the anxiety of failure. I caught myself several times that morning starting to have thoughts of doubt and becoming anxious, but then I looked at the pearl and remembered the advice from the hermit, "Forget not the great heron!"

This day at the beach had started much like the many other days I had enjoyed at the beach. The sun would slowly rise and begin to cook you as the rays of light became more direct. As the noon hour approached, I would begin my ritual. After a three-mile jog and a short swim beyond the breakers, I would then attempt to read the first chapter of my new book.

After reading for a while, I reclined back in my rusty beach chair and fell asleep. Between daydreaming and near full sleep, I imagined walking up those granite steps at the hospital wearing my white coat with pockets full of important notes. My mind wandered without any purpose.

I thought about last week's episode of *Medical Center* on the television. Joe Gannon was the popular doctor who always seemed to have the right answer to every problem that came his way. I imagined how amazing it would be to say, "Give this patient two milligrams of morphine stat, prepare him for surgery, and I will meet you in the OR." I snapped back to reality. My thoughts had been positive, and I was not fixating on rejection. Fantasizing about TV shows may not be what the hermit had in mind, but at least I had avoided thoughts of fear, which had preoccupied me recently. I spent an hour or longer in a semiconscious state, wandering around in the blissful playground of the mind. I was enjoying the gift of tranquility and calmness that only the ocean and its shore can provide.

Then from somewhere behind me, I could faintly hear a familiar voice calling my name. For several seconds, I thought I was dreaming, for I was in that restful state just before falling to sleep. It was easy to doze on a hot, sunny day. But the calling of my name became louder and more distinct. I woke up a bit and opened my eyes. I peered over my shoulder to see if I was hearing voices or just imagining the sounds. It was my father marching directly toward me as if he were on a mission.

For my dad to be on the beach without a fishing pole in his hand, something had to be seriously wrong. I jumped from my chair just as my father reached me on the beach. "Your sister called. She has been trying to reach us for two hours."

"What's wrong?" I interrupted. "Is someone sick? What's the problem?" My father was sweating and a little out of breath. I swept up the beach chair and my belongings, and we hurried back to the camper.

My dad was panting like a dog who had just stopped running after a car. "Your sister says that a medical school called the house this morning and that it was very important that you call them today. I have the number back in the camper. Your sister said it was Miss Simpson, the secretary for Dean Johnston. Do you know who she is talking about?"

With a thousand thoughts running through my mind, we picked up our pace back to the camper. "Yes, I sure do. I spent most of the day with Miss Simpson last week waiting to speak with Dr. Johnston. Remember the hospital that I told you I went to? Remember, I told you I spoke to the man who has the power of the choice? Well, Dean Johnston is that man! How on earth did the call get through to you?"

"Your sister called the phone operator for information for the nearest pay phone to the campground. She was unable to find the number at the front gate to the park. She did find the number of the phone booth next to the camp's shower and restroom facilities. She called the phone booth and let it ring for over twenty minutes before someone picked up the phone and answered it. She said it was an emergency and they should contact the attendant at the front gate to get in touch with me. The message finally got to me a few minutes ago." He was now out of breath. "You need to return the call to the Dean!" All he knew was that Ms. Simpson had said that it was very important that I call her today. No other details were given. When we arrived at the camper, my mom was standing just inside the door, looking out and anxiously awaiting my arrival. She opened the screen door to the camping trailer and with a look of excitement handed me a small piece of paper with the name Ms. Simpson and a long-distance phone number. For a second I stood motionless, staring at the piece of paper in my hand.

My dad nudged my shoulder as if to wake me up. "Well, go call them. There's a pay phone booth at the side of the restroom facilities. Charge the call to our home phone number."

The phone booth was on the sunny side of the building. There was not a cloud in the sky, and the gentle breeze at the shore had no effect on the protected booth that lie in the direct path of the sun's light. As I dialed the operator, I could feel my heart pounding. Sweat dripped from my forehead onto the wrinkled piece of paper. The phone booth was like an oven. Because of the congested beach traffic along the road, I had to close the door to block out the roar of cars passing by. After what seemed like an eternity, the connection was made, and I introduced myself.

Miss Simpson was at her desk when the phone rang, "Hello Charles. It's good to hear from you again. I trust you are having a good day."

I could tell by the inflection of her voice that she was smiling, much like I remembered her from the week before. She had the kind of smile that made her eyes brighten up with happiness.

I was searching for the right response, but maybe because of the pressure of the moment and the unbearable heat of the oven in which I found myself, it was difficult to talk. "It's good to speak with you, too. I was told that you, or rather Dr. Johnston needed to speak with me today?"

37

Miss Simpson was doing everything she could to hold back her emotions. "Yes, let me get him for you. I'll put you on hold, and he will be with you shortly."

It must have been over a hundred degrees in that booth that afternoon. The humidity was especially high, as well. My heart was pounding in my chest. I said to myself, "This is not a good time to become faint."

I opened the door of the booth while waiting and the slight cool of circulating air was a welcome reprieve. Then, there was a voice on the other end, "Hello, I am Dean Johnston. Is this Charles Carpenter?"

As I closed the door to the phone booth, oddly I thought about my grandmother and the smell in her kitchen during those hot summer days when she used to cook cabbage. I was a little boy, no more than ten, but I can recall the odor and how hot her kitchen was without air conditioning. I imagined that my body's entrapment at that moment seemed like that pressure-cooked head of cabbage. I remembered the whistling sound of the cooker when the pressure would rise and then....

In a flash, I returned to the present. "Yes sir, it is. This is Charles." There were several seconds of silence, and it seemed as if I was waiting for the rest of my life to begin. It was one of those moments in time that seemed to stand still. All my senses were maximally fixated and keenly aware and present in the moment. Nothing else in the world mattered. I had no fears. I had no anxiety in my heart. I was totally aware of my presence. I was calm.

(Except, yes, I was hot! And yes, I was sweating profusely!)

His firm voice resonated. One could also appreciate a subtle kindness the tone of his spoken words, "I think I have some good news for you that will make you quite happy. What I am about to say will change your life forever. Charles, we would like for you to join us as a first-year medical student this year." A moment of silence followed. "We had an applicant choose another school yesterday, and an opening became available. I need to know your reply verbally today if you accept this spot in our freshman class. You may know that classes start in less than a week, and I need to know if you can be here at the start of the new school year. If you need to think about this offer, you will need to call me back before 5:30 today."

There was the briefest split second of hesitation. "Sir, I do not need to call you back. I have known the answer to your offer even before I was in your office last week. Yes, yes, yes! I will be there!"

Dr. Johnston chuckled slightly, then returning to his professional manner, he politely shared his welcoming speech which. "We are pleased to have you join us. I look forward to getting to know you over the next four years." He hesitated for a moment. He was going off script, and in a more personable tone, he concluded, "Hold on a bit, and I will connect you with Miss Simpson. She will need to ask you a few questions to get the process rolling."

In a few seconds, a familiar voice was on the other end of the line. There was excitement in her voice. "Well, hey there! So how are you doing now? Are you having a great day or what?"

With a slight crackle in my voice, I told her, "Yes, Miss Simpson, I truly am!"

"I am so excited and proud of you. Please call me Paula from here on out. Now, I must have an address so that I can mail you the acceptance agreement. Please return it as soon as possible by overnight mail. I've got a lot of work to do on my end to get you ready for the next week."

For the first time when talking with Miss Simpson, or Paula as she was now known to me, I found the right words, "I think you have done a lot for me already."

We both laughed, and she began to tell me about the girl from

New Jersey who had received early acceptance back in February. Fortunately for me, at the last minute she had decided that she was better suited to do research; she would be going to graduate school at Harvard to study genetics instead. After giving Paula the information she needed, we said goodbye. Likely, this kind and sympathetic young woman, Paula Simpson, had played a big part in the miracle that had just occurred in my life. By the way she spoke to me, I knew that she was aware of what she had done. And yes, I knew that one simple act of kindness had made all the difference.

I hung up the phone. Now wet with sweat, I slid open the glass panel of the phone booth and welcomed the fresh air. I knelt and laid my head on my knees. My mind was blank. Then I became distinctly aware of the impression of the pearl that was embedded against my skin inside my closed hand. I lifted my head, opened my hand, and remembered that I had taken it from my pocket and put it in my hand just before Miss Simpson answered the phone. I stared at the perfection of the smooth pearl. I smiled as large drops of sweat landed in the palm of my opened hand. I thought about the hermit and all his sage advice.

In a single, confident motion, I jumped from the squatting position on the ground outside of the phone booth. "Is this really happening? This is too good to be true! Yes, it is, and I am ready," I thought. I ran to the camper where my parents were waiting for my return. I told them my unbelievable story, just as it had unfolded. We all three took turns hugging each other. Neither they nor I seemed to notice or even care about the profuse sweat covering my body as we embraced each other. That afternoon, hidden from even the most observant eye, were tears of joy mixed with those beads of sweat that dripped off my cheeks. It was a perfect day. It was a day of abundance!

"You know, you just had a miracle happen in your life," my dad said. I had never seen my dad cry nor heard his voice break with emotion before.

"This is a miracle! Son, you are going to medical school! I've got so much to do. I've got to wash all your clothes, and I only have a week to fatten you up." My mom looked at my dad who now was sitting in the kitchen chair and firmly squeezed his shoulder. "You have to get that old car ready for the trip." Turning to me, an expression of fear came over her face. "Charles, where are you going stay in that big city?"

"Mom don't worry! Everything will work out. I have no idea where I will be living ten days from now." I knew my mom well. When she started to worry, many thoughts began to whirl around in her head, and she would end up doing the "what ifs" (most likely this malady is an inheritable trait), but there was always something I could do that would calm her down and bring her back to reality. I took a step toward her and gave her a big hug. Possibly, all moms are suckers for this tactic. I whispered in her ear, "Everything is going to be just fine. All three of us will do what we must do. Now, you stop worrying." With both arms, I held her away from me and looked into her tearful eyes. "You don't have to fatten me up anymore. These flat dumplings and fried chicken have been putting plenty of pounds on me."

I walked outside the trailer and stared at our campsite. I bent over to stoke the remains of the bonfire from the night before. So many emotions were stirring in me. This was a supernatural event. This was a miracle. You talk about impeccable timing! I could not believe someone would drop out with only a week to go before school starts. Somebody was looking after me. This was possibly the first time in my life that I believed in miracles.

CHAPTER 5
Days of Gratitude

My mother's down east home-cooked meal of stuffed peppers was absolutely the best stuffed peppers that I have ever eaten. The festive air around the lantern-lit picnic table that evening outside the camping trailer most assuredly added to the pure delicacy of the meal. A favorite meal of mine, the dish consists of a piece of American cheese atop a large green pepper filled with a tomato-based rice and hamburger mixture. The softball sized vegetable is baked in an oven, and the cheese turns a golden brown just before being served. Even on its own it is a filling meal.

After dinner, we discussed many of the details that had to be gone over before I left for medical school in less than a week. As expected, my mom was fixated on the wardrobe, "Now, Charles, you must go to the department store when we return home and purchase some new dress shirts. And, oh yes, we need to buy you some new underwear. Yours are looking a bit thread worn." She quickly qualified her response. "You know, I *have* been washing them all summer long, and a mother does notice these things."

My dad jumped in, "Son, we've got to get the oil changed in your car. And has the medical school talked to you about a student loan? Tuition for medical school has to be pretty hefty!" This kind of question was a specialty of my dad's—perhaps of all fathers.

He always worried about money. My whole life I had heard him qualify all of my activities with familiar words, "Are you sure you have enough money?"

I remembered something that the dean had shared. I replied, "The school will help me set that all up during the first week of classes." I smiled at him. I knew he needed reassurance. "You know something dad, I am not going to worry about the cost of my medical education. The important thing is that I made it. I got in!

This may be the first time in my life that I could honestly say that I am not worried about the cost of getting through the next four years." These words seemed to relieve my dad of his anxiety for the moment. Without even questioning the effect that the words would have on him I carried on, "I wonder how much an embroidered white lab coat will cost? I think I will buy two, so I'll always have one clean."

"I like that!" my mom chimed in as she started to wash the dishes that were piled up in the tiny sink of the trailer.

"Yep, I think I'll go buy a new red paisley tie for you and get the oil changed when we get home," my dad said. "You know you're not going to have time to go shopping or get any car work done before you leave." He picked up the newspaper from the folding table next to him and started to read.

Later that evening, we began to reflect on the many caring people who had helped me along my way. My parents suggested that I should call them and share with them my good fortune. I do not remember what hour I finally fell asleep that night. I do remember waking up the next morning completely refreshed. I jumped out of bed with much spring to my step. It seemed as if a large weight had been lifted from my shoulders.

This being my last day at the beach for the summer, I knew it would be the last calm and peaceful day that I would see for a long time. I thought about taking one more relaxing stroll down the beach, but I realized that there was something more important that had to be done before leaving. There was one person I must inform about the phone call and my good fortune. Undoubtedly, the wise old beach hermit would be quite pleased about the phone call that changed my life.

During the waning days of August, a day at the beach can become sticky with the high humidity, and a summer breeze is like a gift. Although the trek across the sand dunes and through the maritime forest would be exhausting, my heart was full of joy and my gait light of step. After helping my parents prepare the camping trailer for the trip back home, I started my walk to the home of the hermit. I wanted to tell him that his advice about remaining positive with one's thoughts had worked. The hermit had given me a wonderful gift: a lesson in life, a testament that could be used whenever times got tough. He, too, had a part to play in this miracle that was unfolding in my life.

It is courteous to call beforehand when visiting someone, but with the hermit that was impossible. Besides, it was my belief that he did enjoy my presence; he was rather talkative and very gracious during my past visit. Walking down the shoreline, I noticed that the pelicans were particularly active and even seemed happy when diving for their morning snack of fish. There were no more dead seagulls along the water's edge, and the smell of the ocean's breeze was quite pleasant today. The hermit's advice had proven to be correct about accepting things as they happen and letting your thoughts lead you to your own successes. Perhaps the hermit had learned this lesson about life by sitting at this very shoreline, watching the pelicans at work and play. I am certain that the hermit had learned that the answers to life's mysteries are all around us. All it takes is patience, a discerning eye, and a sense of awareness to unravel these truths.

My visit with the hermit would have to be brief. I imagined that this was the time of the year when he was busy in his garden.

It was harvest season, and all his staples needed to be prepared for the winter months ahead.

I approached from the north through the maritime forest, and since the wind was coming off the ocean, the horse flies would not be a concern. Sure enough, as I had predicted, when I arrived the hermit was busy tending to the remaining harvest from his garden. Without hesitation, he stood up and greeted me. I was pleased that he gave me a big bear hug when he heard of my good fortune. He did not seem surprised; rather, he was purely joyous.

Still, he quickly returned to his work. "It will rain tomorrow, and this crop of pole beans and corn must be harvested today," he said as he continued to pick his vegetables.

"He who gathers in summer is a wise son.

He who sleeps in harvest is a son who causes shame."

I offered to help him to pick his crop, but he declined, pushing my hands away, "Your hands have a different harvest to gather."

He seemed preoccupied with the gathering of his vegetables. "You know, the change in the season is only a few weeks away. The peak in hurricane season is September 15th. There is much to do in anticipation of a storm." Respecting his concerns, we kept the visit brief and said our farewells. However, just as I was leaving, I asked him if he would like a gift upon my return, "Lima beans would grow very well next summer in this garden."

He stopped his work and appeared to be reaching for his next thought. "There is a book that you may want to read and then bring upon your return. It's called the *Tao Te Ching*. It is a collection of the writings of Lao Tsu who was an older contemporary of Confucius in the sixth century B.C. The essence of Taoism is contained in the spiritual writing. ,There is one particular passage that you must learn. It will broaden your knowledge in preparation for your new harvest."

With that inspiring request, I left the hermit to tend his crop, and I was off to my new life in the big city where untold adventures awaited my arrival.

I made my way back to the camping site and found my parents packed and ready to go. We piled into the truck, pulling the trailer behind. As we entered our hometown, I had a passing thought about my high school football coach, Mr. McFarland. He was one of the people who had helped me along the way. We had remained in touch throughout college. I remember the pep talk he gave as we were about to run onto the field at the start of the state championship playoffs, "Boys be proud and enjoy the moment when you stand atop the mountain of success. In each of your lives, you will have some victories. Enjoy the moments of glory. But, remember that fame and success are fleeting. Remember that life's trophies will take wings. In the passing of time, they will be lost and forgotten. Remember, the hard times as well. They are the most helpful in making you champions."

His words were well received then, and his wisdom rang true even now as we drove through our small hometown. A football coach is like a father. He is a friend but also a teacher whom you come to respect and hold dear throughout your lifetime. Again today, I truly felt like a champion. My football, both on and off the field, had been tremendously helpful. It seemed like only yesterday that I was playing football with all my teammates. Today seemed like a good day for reminiscing.

I knew that the good news would spread quickly among my family and friends. There would be many people to visit before leaving on my great adventure.

Upon arriving home, many details about my move to the medical center had to be resolved. In just two days, I had to decide where I would live in the city. It was a city of several hundred thousand people; it would be quite different from the town where

I grew up. Finding a safe and convenient home where I would live for the next four years would be a critical choice.

I only knew one person in the city near the medical school: my college roommate's girlfriend. I was hoping that she might be able to help me find a place to stay on such short notice.

So, I called her, and she suggested that I reach out to her mother who still lived in the city. She gave me the number, and I called her mother, Mabel Levine. She did not answer, so I left a message. Fortunately, that evening, she did return the call, and she was excited to hear that I would be moving to her city and starting medical school. As it turned out, she had an upstairs room in her house that she had been considering renting to a medical student. In the past, she was a bit leery in doing this because she did not know any of the students. However, knowing that I was a friend of her daughter's and that we both had gone to the same college, she felt quite comfortable in allowing me to rent the upstairs room in her house.

She told me the house was in a quiet, comfortable community only three blocks from the medical school. Mrs. Levine, a widow, lived on the first floor of her home and rarely needed to go upstairs. Since both of her children had moved out, she was quite certain that the living conditions would be suitable for someone who had to do a lot of studying. And so, good fortune continued for me and the problem of where to stay was quickly resolved.

Choosing what to pack for my new home and traveling the three-hundred-and-fifty miles was also important. Because I would be traveling in a small car, it was necessary to decide what to leave behind.

My wardrobe was packed into four suitcases, which were crammed into the back seat, and my radio, clock, desk chair, study lamp, and other conveniences of living made it into the trunk of the car. Fortunately, my bike also made the trip on its carrier hitched on the back of the car.

The morning of departure came, and I suspected it would be an awkward, emotional moment for both my parents and me. I remembered just four years before when I left home for college — the tears running down my mom's cheeks and my dad pacing and nervously patting his fingers upon the car fender. So, not wanting to go through such an emotional scene for a second time, I decided to confront the present unfolding of farewell gestures by addressing the past. "OK, Mom and Dad, I am not your little boy leaving home for the first time. I'm all grown up this time. So, no one is going to get all emotional and cry, right? And besides, I'm off this time to learn to be a physician."

They both laughed, and my mom gave me a hug. "Study hard," she said. My dad patted me on the back. Like most fathers, he was a man of few words.

My mature and up-front approach to the potential awkward moment had worked. And so, I was off to begin my new journey, or at least I thought I was. However, as I was backing out of the driveway, my mom came running to the driver's side of the car, "Charles, you forgot your watch!"

I stopped the car, reached for my watch, and she leaned inside the car and gave me a soft kiss on my cheek. Mostly hidden, except for my discerning eye, there on my mother's cheek was the wet trace of a tear. She backed away from the car, walked back to the porch, and waved goodbye. As I was turning off our street onto the road, I looked into my rearview mirror and noticed that my parents were still standing on the front porch. Dad had his arm around my mom's shoulders, and she was (as I expected) wiping away tears. I waved my hand out the side window and quickly disappeared from their sight. I thought to myself that the love from parents is truly a gift that never stops and gives you strength to face the challenges that lie ahead.

I drove slowly through my small town that morning. I was neither sad nor melancholy but reflective and thankful for the fulfilling memories this little town had given me during my youth.

There on the left was the little league baseball field where I once played. I remembered that one crowning moment when I hit a ball hard enough that it bounced over the center field fence for a stand-up double. I always wanted to hit one over the fence for a home run but never did. Yes, I really would like to have known what it would feel like to hit a home run. Even though I have not picked up a bat in four years, in my heart, I still keep trying to hit that home run.

I slowed down as I rode past the high school practice football field. There, standing on the five-man blocking sled was Coach McFarland, blowing his whistle, and running his new players through the drills. I remembered that the last weeks in August, just before the first game of the year, we had morning and afternoon practices each day. In so doing, we avoided the heat of the day. They still were tough. I guess they did work to build character and muscle. I wanted to stop and say goodbye to my coach, but he had wished me well by phone the day before. Besides, just like me, he had his own new challenges ahead.

As I drove out of town, I wondered, "Is it hard to go back and relive the past? Is the present all that we have? Is the future the only thing we can attempt to change? Where have I heard these words before?" The thoughts of the hermit kept returning to me. I then questioned, "Who is in control? Is there a plan for everyone? Are the events in our lives according to our will? Do miracles really occur? Seems like I just received one!" There were so many unanswered questions. "I wonder if I am the only one who asks all these questions?"

As I was passing through the last stoplight in my town, I suddenly remembered when I was sixteen and had earned my license to drive. At this very intersection, I drove through a red light, and I rear-ended another car, spinning me around. No one was hurt, but it did scare me. It also taught me a great lesson—not to daydream when performing a task. I had to go to court, and I will never forget the judge pointing his finger at me and admonishing me to, "Stay focused, son!"

Finally, I was on the highway, at cruising speed, on my way to my new life and new career. I had so many questions about life. I smiled and thought to myself about these three distinct memories and the life lessons that my hometown had taught me: never stop dreaming, and never stop trying; hard work, determination, and some skill can lead to ultimate success; and finally, life will have some bumps along the way, and though we may get knocked off course slightly, always stay focused.

Farewell parents. Farewell little league field. Farewell coach. Farewell traffic court judge. Farewell hometown! I am off to become a physician!

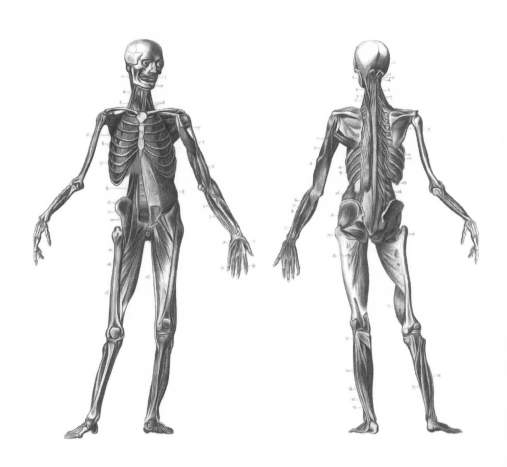

CHAPTER 6

The Body and It's Many Parts

The auditorium on the main floor of the medical school was adorned with theater seating and state of the art projection systems. Seventy-six first year medical students had come together for our first class, an orientation concerning our next four years of medical training. The dean of the medical school would give the presentation. I sat several rows from the back of the auditorium so that I could observe all the activity taking place. Some of the students were well tanned and casually dressed, appearing as if they had enjoyed the summer and now were well rested for the ordeal to come. Several others anxiously walked out of the auditorium to visit the restroom and empty their nervous bladders one final time before the convening of the lecture. Most of us sat quietly with new writing pads and pens waiting diligently to take notes. The room was full of tense excitement.

For me, the past two weeks were likely the most exciting in my life. Now, this moment, I was sitting here as *one* of the seventy-six students in the freshman class. Questions were racing through my mind. Had I studied enough? Was I as smart as the other seventy-five? Was I prepared for the challenge ahead? Could I keep up the pace of the long hours of studying and give up my play time of watching TV and exercising? Did I have the determination to make it to the end? I took a deep breath as the lights dimmed. From the left side of the stage, the dean of the medical school entered looking regal. Day one of medical school had now begun!

He spoke for a little over an hour. Mostly he addressed the rules, regulations, and expectations placed upon us. The last ten minutes, he opened up for discussion and entertained questions from the class. Someone from the front of the room (the guy with the nervous bladder, I think) asked the dean if he had any advice that would give him an edge and set him on the path of success in medical school. I noted that the dean thought for a moment, formed his response, and with a devilish grin on his face responded, "Having comfortable living quarters and a quiet place to sleep is essential while in medical school. If you are married, having an understanding spouse would make a huge difference in the quality of your life. Your spouse can be your most important asset or your worst nightmare." With that, he left the stage. A financial officer for the school spoke briefly and asked if there were any questions regarding the payment plan that was sent to our homes in July. I had no idea what he was talking about. In July, all I did was walk to a mailbox and open letters of rejection. "I guess this financial officer will realize that I'm here and haven't sent in a cent toward my education," I thought. Then, a startling thought came to my mind, "Oh no! My dad is going to go to the mailbox and find a bill from the school and freak out! I better call him tonight and prepare him. Hmm, or maybe the financial office will never know I am here. Ok, I need to make an appointment this afternoon and remind them of the circumstances surrounding my last minute acceptance."

The gathering promptly ended, and we all exited the auditorium somewhat more prepared for the next day. As I was leaving, I reflected what the dean had said. I had been mesmerized by his thick black eyebrows; they seemed to move precisely to accentuate his profound recommendations. It was rumored around school that he was once a teenage movie star who gave up the Hollywood glitter to become an internationally renowned and respected neurologist. We all took his words as gospel.

And so, I had survived the first day of medical school. Unwittingly, I had already followed the dean's advice of having a quiet place to study, and I was looking forward to returning to my place of refuge. As far as a spouse was concerned, I was pleased that I did not have to worry about that. Fortunately, now, there was neither a wife nor a serious girlfriend that would be taking time away from my studies.

As I had looked around the auditorium that day, I thought I could identify several married students by the panic that darkened their faces when they imagined the demands awaiting them upon return home in the evenings to come. Each would likely be greeted by their spouse and would be asked for an accounting of the day. Their spouses would want to talk and have quality time together. The medical student would want to eat his meal and rest for a bit in quiet solitude. He would then open the books and study the chapters for the next day's lectures. This student had already listened to, analyzed, or written down 10,000 words or more of notes for the day; the spouse was ready to speak 10,000 more! The spouse had waited all day for the student's return, and the need for social interaction was high. The medical student was seeking solitude. Herein, lay the conflict that would await the married student each day. Yes, I could imagine the increased stress that married life could add to the already overflowing plate of the first-year medical student. Granted, an understanding and sympathetic spouse could be an asset. A friend to share the journey would be nice. But for me, I looked forward to the late-night solitude in my quiet room with only a three-inch thick gross anatomy book for my companion.

There are many rites of passage one must pass in order to be successful in your career and happy with your life as a medical student. Learning the science of medicine and becoming a physician has its unique pathways that every student must follow. First, each student must take many preparatory science classes before getting to medical school. Many animals had to be dissected and good grades earned in order to move on. In the past, there were frogs, rabbits, cats, dogs and the well-known guinea pig to dissect. So, to now arrive in medical school and to have in front of you the grand finale, the human cadaver, awaiting the meticulous cut from your scalpel is truly a wonderful rite of passage for every young doctor in training. The first four months of each student's career are quite similar, involving sixteen plus hours a week in the anatomy lab, learning methodical dissection. In time, the magnificent form and mechanics of the human body will be displayed, eventually understood, and put to memory. Each student will have dissected the human form into its smallest parts. It is important that each part retains its relationship to the other. In doing so, the complexity of the human body is appreciated, and its form and function becomes truly awe-inspiring. And, to think that one must commit this vast knowledge to memory is a daunting feat. This rite of passage can be a nightmare, sometimes overwhelming and terrifying.

Our Chief of Anatomy, Dr. Adolf Bourne, did not make this any easier. He employed torturous techniques of teaching.

Monday through Thursday from one to five p.m., each first-year student had his hands literally inside the body of their cadaver. Each week saw the start of a new organ system and the fine points of each structure. The dissecting hall held twenty-six tables lined up in three long rows. Atop the heavy metal four by six-foot table laying face up was a human body. Three medical students were assigned to each body. The remaining table was reserved for graduate students in anatomy. We were told that one day they would be teaching medical students. They were very good at dissecting and often we would go to them for help when we were lost, literally, deep in a body.

The professors would walk around each table and help with

the dissection, answer students' questions, and ask his own questions to stimulate further dissection. The afternoons went by quickly. The pace at which we dissected each body system seemed equally rapid.

Then, the dreaded Friday would come at the end of every week of study. Fridays were known as the "Gestapo" session with Adolf. About every twenty minutes or so, two or three students would be called into the back room. The back room was Dr. Bourne's private dissecting lab where upon a table would lie his perfectly dissected cadaver. Once the door was closed, the questioning session would begin wherein the first student and each consecutive student would be asked a question. Each question would have three parts. The first question asked was a general question about the function of a certain body part that had been studied that week. The second and third questions were progressively harder to answer. You were never given the correct answers during the session. We would learn, however, as the months progressed that if you answered a question favorably, Dr. Bourne would just look over his glasses and say, "Hmmm," and proceed to the next question.

If, by chance, you stumbled on the first or second question, your life at that moment would become considerably more unpleasant. Most of your classmates outside of the closed door would hear Professor Bourne's booming voice as he firmly repeated the question to the student. We learned quickly that the best way to answer a question was with as much precision and confidence as was possible. Any reply given weakly or showing evidence of insecurity was considered by Dr. Bourne as ignorance. Eventually each student would leave the room exhausted but relieved knowing that they had survived another week of anatomy.

However, if you had done poorly, you were invited to return to his private dissecting chamber on Saturday morning and given a chance to prove your working knowledge of that week's organ system. About half of the class would visit Dr. Bourne in his back chambers weekly, and there were always a half a dozen or so that, unfortunately, were back for the revisit on Saturday morning. This often meant another six or so hours would be spent in the anatomy lab Friday evening preparing for the next day's ordeal. Usually one of graduate students in anatomy would be assigned to the anatomy lab Friday night and would spend one-on-one time with the endangered medical students.

To be clear, this was not the way any medical student ever wanted to spend a Friday evening.

Friday night was one of the few down times a student had, and we all looked forward to gathering at the Rosebud Tavern, which was a city block away from the school. Fortunately, I was never asked to return to the follow-up Gestapo sessions on a Saturday morning and, therefore, do not have a firsthand account of this ordeal, but it was rumored throughout the class that it was both humiliating and pressure packed. We learned quickly as the week came to its closure you should be well-prepared for anatomy class on Friday afternoons.

However, I do have one vivid memory of a Friday afternoon session with Dr. Bourne that brought me quite close to sharing a Saturday morning in his private chambers.

That day I recall that Dr. Bourne was in one of his rare and clever moods. "Let's talk about the thumb today. Mr. Carpenter, we all know that the thenar muscles work the thumb. Name me the muscles that make up the thenar imminence and their functions and innervations," he challenged.

I took a second to think. I was determined to answer with confidence, "The three muscles of the thenar imminence are the abductor pollicis brevis, the flexor pollicis, and the opponens pollicis. They are all innervated by the median nerve. " I stumbled for a moment but then remembered their functions, "The first abducts, the second flexes, and the third ..." and for a second my mind went blank. Dr. Bourne looked over his glasses and stared into my eyes. "The opponens pollicis brings the thumb across the fingers as to touch the fingers in a pinching manner?"

Dr. Bourne was expressionless, "So is it true to say that the action of the thumb is generated by the intact functioning of the median nerve?"

Now, the second question was always the one that tricked you up and made you fall if you jumped too fast. I thought for a moment to form my answer, "No, because another movement of the thumb is to adduct, that is to move the thumb into the palm of the hand, and this muscle is innervated by the ulnar nerve!"

Adolf smiled but knew that he may finally have me in his baited trap with the next question. And with that, he stuck his thumb straight up into the air, "Good job, Charles!" It was totally out of character.

Then the smile vanished from his face, and he began to whisper, "Would I be able to give you this thumbs up sign if an attacker slashed my forearm across my distal radius?"

The moment I took to think must have seemed like an eternity to Dr. Bourne, "Son, do you have an answer to the question?"

I collected my thoughts, "The cut across your radius would sever the radial nerve, and the radial nerve innervates the adductor pollicis longus and the extensor pollicis brevis and longus, all of which would be responsible for sticking the thumb straight up into the air." Then with confidence I took the bait on the hook, "No, you would not be able to give me the thumbs up sign."

I will never forget his cocky tone when he knew he was right. "Wrong! Your thinking is correct. Anatomy is not just memorizing the names of the many parts of the body; it's also about how each individual part relates to the other and how they function together." Then with a comforting smile, he placed his hand in the air with thumbs up sign, "You were very close. You almost had it right."

Then he proceeded on and drilled another student, never giving me the correct answer. Each student left the room that day with their own little pearl of anatomical wisdom. We had all become more inquisitive than ever. That evening, after several hours of review, it finally came to me. There is a nerve branching from the median nerve that innervates all of these extensor muscles of the thumb, and it does this just below the elbow, a long way from the cut lower down on the forearm just above the wrist. The professor was right in that he would have been able to give the thumbs up sign weakly since the enervation of the muscle was intact. The location of parts relative to each other was critical. Dr. Bourne must have been satisfied even though I did not answer the third question correctly because I was not asked to return for a follow-up session on Saturday morning.

The detail of the human body is breathtaking. Having learned so much about its parts took tremendous determination. It also took a lot of discipline, sacrificing the pleasures of TV, movies, playing sports, or just going for a walk. I thought about the 2,000 applicants who did not get accepted. Many of them were well educated and deserved to have been accepted in a medical school. My journey was worth any cost. The first semester of the first year of medical school can be summed up in four words: details, determination, discipline, and duty.

Weeks of lectures, labs, and study marched on for the four months until Christmas. The time flew by, but I was ready for the drive home for Christmas break. There were only happy memories of Christmas past. Each year added new and exciting times to be shared. After what I had just endured, I imagined that this holiday would be even more special.

CHAPTER 7

The Smells of Christmas

As I drove home those three hundred and fifty miles, my thoughts became more focused on the pleasures of Christmas. "The break away from the books will be great, and my mom's cooking will be a real treat," I thought to myself.

Suddenly it dawned on me: I had forgotten an important part of Christmas. "Here I am, riding home, Christmas is three days away. I will have a joyful family waiting to give me their hero's welcome, and I have not bought one Christmas present!" I laughed at myself and thought about all of those young men you see in the stores on December 24th. In near panic they would be buying their last-minute gifts. "Am I joining their ranks? At least I had a good excuse." There had been absolutely no time to think about Christmas, much less shop, until now.

In a town of 15,000 people, change does not happen quickly. Christmas lights were wound around each light pole down Main Street. The water tower, high above, had its lighted star atop. It had been this way as long as I could remember. In the middle of town, would be Santa's hut where all the parents would stop with their children to meet Santa and share their Christmas lists.

Returning home from the big city, the streets seemed a little narrower and the main street a little shorter than in the past. The store fronts, brightly decorated for Christmas, seemed a little more run down and their paint a little more faded. I thought about the many memories of my hometown; it seemed in the past that it never changed, but now the changes were evident.

Then, I turned onto my street. I knew my parents would be anticipating my return. I knew in my heart what awaited me. The small house would be clean and tidy. The smell of several of my favorite Christmas treats would be in the air as I opened the door. The tree would be neatly trimmed with all the same ornaments we hung for the past twenty years. And all the presents would be neatly wrapped and placed under the tree.

I thought to myself, "Parents are so predictable." My mom would say, as she kissed me on the cheek, "You're looking skinny. Are you eating right? Now, you go sit down in the living room and I'll bring you something to eat."

My dad would be sitting in his blue recliner with his TV remote nearby, his scanner squawking in the background with reports of happenings in the county. It would not take long for him to pop the much anticipated question, "How have you been son? How's the money holding out?" After looking up from reading his paper and glancing directly at me, he would have something to say about my appearance, "Your hair is getting too long."

I finally arrived home, and the house had aged, but otherwise it was unchanged. The side-porch light was on, and there behind the storm door my mom stood awaiting my arrival. Thereafter, the events unfolded as I had predicted. The tree was perfectly displayed with its presents neatly arrayed below. Remarks of weight loss and too long hair followed. The scanner in the background reported that a car had been pulled over with a broken taillight. My father asked how the money was holding out.

Within minutes of arriving home, upon my lap sat a large plate of my favorite home-cooked Christmas treats. My mouth watered when I saw my favorite Christmas candy, butter cream candies, flavored with almond, covered with chocolate, and topped with a walnut. They did not serve this in the hospital cafeteria!

I was not disappointed with the predictable flow of the holidays. Some things are not meant to change. However, after being away for four months, subtle things do change, like the aging that naturally occurs upon the faces of those you love. No doubt, they likely saw the wear and tear upon my own face. This Christmas, there was one obviously glaring difference that made me take notice and think.

As I sat eating my much-loved Christmas goodies, I realized that I really couldn't taste them. The butter cream candies looked delicious as always, but they tasted the same as the food in the hospital cafeteria. Everything tasted the same.

My mom and dad sat in their matching blue lazy boy chairs, and we talked about the first semester. Neither of them spoke overtly about their feelings; however, I could tell that they were proud. I had not seen that look for a long time. It made me happy. Their smiles of joy and pride made for an especially nice little Christmas present. It made the past semester, spending all those hours inside a cadaver, that much more meaningful.

The next day seemed to unfold in the usual order of a traditional Christmas morning. Before we exchanged gifts around the tree, I walked to the kitchen and picked up two warm-from-the-oven, homemade cinnamon buns and devoured them. Something puzzled me, as I returned to the living room to start handing out gifts from under the tree. I realized that the cinnamon buns tasted like everything else I had just eaten. When it was my turn to open presents, I started to unwrap the first one, and to my astonishment, I noticed the paper did not feel right. I couldn't find, just by touch, the end of the paper to begin unwrapping my gift. I was baffled by the lack of senses that I was experiencing.

I began to laugh. My parents looked at me as if I had lost my mind. "Charles, what are you laughing at?"

"My fingers are pickled!" I looked at my parents to see if they understood what I was talking about. "It's the formaldehyde from the cadaver; my hands have been in his body for four months. I noticed last night that I couldn't really taste the Christmas treats. They all tasted the same. Just now, I realized that I couldn't quite feel the paper wrapping on this gift. The formaldehyde has numbed my sense of touch, as well as my taste."

"Did you not wear gloves?"

"Of course I did, Mom, but they only last for thirty minutes before they dry out, get hard, and crack. You get focused on what you're doing, and you just keep working with your fingers exposed. We all did. Mom, I know you are going to be upset with that. Over the past three weeks when finals were coming, things got pretty intense. I was so focused on studying and getting through tests that I did not stop to think about it." My mom's jaw dropped in amazement. "You know, come to think about it, driving home yesterday, the steering wheel even felt different in my hands."

Then with his characteristic wit, my father attempted to ask, "Well son, did you have problems when you went to the…"

My mom interjected before he could finish, "Now George, its Christmas morning! You be good!"

We all laughed. I did share that it had been "a little difficult" to take care of personal hygiene. My dad was always humorous, especially when he could embarrass someone. "You know, your mom and I have wondered what that odd smell is on you. We first noticed it as soon as you walked in the door two days ago. It's strong! Can't you smell it?"

I was surprised. "Actually, I did smell it everywhere I went, up until about a month ago, then it went away, and I assumed it was gone. But come to think of it, I can't remember smelling anything lately, the past several weeks really. Everything I eat tastes like cardboard. In fact, these cinnamon rolls look scrumptious, but their taste is not how I remembered them."

My dad hooted with laughter, "Your nose is pickled too!"

He was right. Dr. Bourne had warned us about a month ago when some of the students were getting nosebleeds that we should use Vaseline inside our nostrils to protect them from the inhalation of the formaldehyde fumes. My nose had not bled, but it did itch all the time. My olfactory mucosa had been preserved with formaldehyde and my sense of smell numbed temporarily.

That night like always, the Christmas meal of turkey, dressing, mashed potatoes, lima beans, and homemade yeast rolls were piled upon my plate. Everything looked as delectable as always, but for me, the taste was a little flat this year.

This experience, perhaps common to all first semester medical students, is funny to look back on, but none of us want to relive it. It would be a unique occurrence and lasting lesson. In my case, it was a once in a lifetime Christmas, for every Christmas thereafter, the taste of the almond buttercream candy returned and became the hallmark of each Christmas for me.

The Christmas season for a first-year medical student is a unique experience. The hometown seems a little smaller. The parents seem a little older. True, the events surrounding your life for the past four months have taken away your senses of smell, taste, and touch; the sights and sounds of Christmas, however seemed intensified. This Christmas is a passing moment, a rite of passage (if you will) in the life of a medical student.

Nothing can take away the magical feeling of family unity and Christmas spirit. In its own way, it brings carefree happiness, unusual laughter, and a unique smell and taste to the holiday season.

As this Christmas day ended, after unwrapping all the gifts, I had a moment of quiet. I reflected on the wealth of new knowledge I had acquired. I looked at the loved ones surrounding me. Even though he was aging, I could imagine the innerworkings of my dad's magnificent body. There are so many muscles. There are so many nerves. Each body part has a name, and they all work in relation to each other. I sat in my living room with an under-standing and appreciation for all the intriguing minutia that makes him a normal human being. This was a moment of awe. Never again in my life, would all this knowledge feel so fresh. This was a beautiful revelation. It was a feeling hard to explain. I thought, "I know all the parts of the body. I can name them." There was only one problem. Next semester, I would start to learn how diseases cause havoc on this miraculous body, and I had been told it would take a lifetime to learn how to treat all these ailments. I had so much more to learn!

CHAPTER 8

A Time of Replenishing

The lima bean seeds were easy to find; the book entitled *Tao Te Ching*, on the other hand, I could only find in an old bookstore in a neighboring town. The day before I returned to school was bitter cold. It was the only day I had free to go visit the hermit. So, with the gifts he requested and a piece of my mom's apple pie in hand, I took off in search of my friend, the recluse who lived deep in the maritime forest. What a contrast the winter made since I last visited his ocean side home. The sand was hot to the feet last summer. Now, a light dusting of fine snow had fallen in the early morning hours. The sand above the tideline was frozen, crackling and crunching as I walked on it. The leaves of the scrubs that were alive and green last summer had turned ochre and tawny. Only an occasional squawk of a lone seagull, aloft in flight, broke the whistling of the blustery, cutting wind whipping off the ocean. The combination of dry snow and sand striking your cold cheeks was stinging.

I chose to enter the hermit's encampment from the south, traveling the path through the swallow between the sand dunes of the maritime forest. With less underbrush to navigate in the winter, the trip to the hermit's home seemed shorter this time.

Perhaps, it was the anticipation of seeing him again or maybe the cold wind, but I found myself almost running down the path toward his pillbox dwelling. What words of advice would I receive from him? I was eager to share with him my excitement about medical school. I would tell him that I survived gross anatomy, and the only adverse outcome was the mummified epidermis of my fingers. Finally, I crested the last sand dune before my destination. I traversed the downward slope that opened to the secluded retreat, and there standing in front of the heavy metal door was the hermit, as if he had anticipated my arrival. He greeted me as I entered the rectangular courtyard, "Welcome back, friend! Come and sit by the fire, and you can explain that big smile on your face. Is it not the first branch of the trigeminal nerve that allows you to do so?"

My eyes widened. How did he know about the enervation of the face? However, I had to immediately correct him! My smile broadened as I politely responded, "Let me correct you. It's the oral group of the facial nerve that enervates the risorius muscle that allow me to lift the corners of my mouth into this smile on my face."

With that, the hermit bowed his head in submission and gave me a huge bear hug. "Welcome back to this place, one can see that the young gentleman is now also a scholar. The correction is accepted."

We sat on the stumps near the fire pit. I handed him the slice of apple pie, and he placed it over the glowing embers to warm it up before digging in. He wiped a few crumbs from his beard and smiled, "Thank your mom for this wonderful pie."

I could tell that he was well prepared for the winter cold. He had replaced the wide-brimmed, straw hat of the summer for a raccoon-skin skull cap that covered his ears and the back of his neck. A long trench coat discarded by a stranger now had deer skin sewn into it. His pants were covered with a patchwork of deer skin, as well. It appeared that the skin of a pelican's throat pouch covered his high-topped shoes, which kept his feet warm and waterproof. I noticed that he had lost that bronze glow to his face from the summer sun. Now, his cheeks were a grayish color, similar to the camouflage of the plant life surrounding his encampment.

It was the seeds that he took joy in as he squeezed them in his fisted hands. "It is with these that life will be renewed in the coming months."

"The forest looks so dead in the winter. It used to be so green, and all of the living creatures were scurrying about. It seems so lifeless at this time of the year," I remarked.

"You see, son, there is not as much gloom as you would imagine. Yes, many creatures are hibernating. The cycle of life would not be complete without the winter. On the beach in winter, the nor'easters blow, and the storm surge pummels the weak dunes and peels away the driftwood and grass. All this debris forms a flotsam, which slowly decays and will replenish the sand with nourishment for the new baby creatures that will be born in March and April.

"Similarly, on the salt marsh the cord grass dies creating peat from the rotten stems that will fertilize the plankton in the spring. The brackish slurry you see in the marsh, its decomposing grass and dead animal matter in a solution of algae and bacteria. Biologists call this detritus. Think of it as nature's soup of nourishment for all the salt marsh organisms waiting to be born by the hundreds of millions just a few months from now. A wise man has observed that..." He had to catch his breath before he could continue...

"'There is time for everything and a season for every activity under heaven. There is a time to be born and a time to die.'"

The hermit took a moment to collect his thoughts. A stern expression overtook him, "The book that you have there in your hand, the *Tao Te Ching*, has provided for over 2500 years a major influence in Chinese thought and culture. Lao Tsu says:

'Many things rise and fall while you watch their return.
They grow and flourish and return to the source.
Returning to the source, they become still, and this is the
way of nature.
The way of nature is unchanging and knowing this is
insight.
When you see this consistency, you will open the mind.
When you open your mind, you will open your heart.
When you become open hearted, you become royal.
And when you become royal, you become close to the
divine.'"

He became still and silent, then intently peered at me, "Did you read this book at all?"

He could see me squirm as I sat on the stump. "Really, I have had no time to read anything other than medical textbooks. I only bought this book yesterday. I have only glanced at it as I was walking here."

He returned to his previous conversation and continued to speak of this cycle of life, of winter and death and replenishing. Then we both became silent, much like nature itself in the winter.

"Our conversation, when we were first together revealed that in life there will be struggles. Was it not said that this struggling was the human way?" He asked.

"Next semester, I will learn about this struggle of man against disease.. We will begin the study of pathology and learn about the many illnesses that affect mankind."

"If one never became sick, had days when he felt badly, then he would never appreciate the wonderful days of splendor. You see, the whole of nature beats like a rhythm of polarity, or opposites. There must be darkness to appreciate light. There must be valleys to understand the challenge of climbing the mountains. If one never experiences winter, then summer days would have no meaning. All living creatures are born, and unfortunately all must anticipate death."

The fire popped several times and broke the momentary silence. "Wouldn't it be nice though, if we never had to suffer?" I mused. "When I become a physician, I will be able to limit the discomfort that comes with illness or injury. After all, is that not the purpose of becoming a doctor, so that you can help people have a happier life by reducing the misery of pain and suffering?"

The hermit reached for a long fire stick, stirred the fire, and added two more sticks of sea oak to the blaze. "It's true that you will undoubtedly learn much about the science of medicine over the next four years. But, over your lifetime you will master the art of medicine as well. You will come to appreciate the nature of man. You will, hopefully, become wise. Knowing how to use your wisdom correctly will also make you compassionate. Caring for the suffering requires both wisdom and compassion."

The hermit looked around and stretched out his arms to his surroundings. "The reason for this existence, why one lives in the maritime forest alone for these many years is to live in touch with nature. By observing these plants and animals, one can also arrive at a deeper understanding of the nature of mankind."

The hermit sat down upon the other stump. With his body becoming rigid, he stared straight into my eyes and pointed to the sky, "The marsh hawk, like many migrating birds flies south for the winter seeking better feeding grounds. They, like we humans, yearn for pleasures. In the summer, the rabbits run frantically from their predators, the ospreys that soar in the sky. This becomes a reminder for humans. They seek out the many pleasures in life but also run from many dangers.

"However, where humans differ from the marsh hawk and the rabbits is that they learn lessons about life. When men search for pleasures, as well as avoid the many dangers surrounding them, they become aware of impermanence. What is impermanence? It is that constantly changing environment in which all creatures live. It means simply, that nothing ever stays the same. All living creatures are in a state of flux, constantly changing day by day and even moment by moment. Their health can change quickly. Their environment can change from hot to cold in a matter of hours. One missed step along the path of life, an acute injury occurs, and a life can worsen irreversibly. A tornado can destroy someone's home and possessions without warning. Human emotions, thoughts, and behaviors can readily be altered by circumstances and changing relationships with others. Men constantly seek pleasures. They avoid change, if possible. Ultimately, they conclude that they have little control over their lives. Men conclude that if one is born, one matures, and one ages. Everyone learns that in the cycle of life all must die. Just like the marsh grass, in the spring of one's life, one sprouts and grows tall. Then in the winter of life, one withers, fades in color, and ultimately dies."

The hermit could not stop himself from chuckling. "Fortunately, somewhere between these two seasons people reproduce and a new generation continues the cycle. To cope with this sullen, downcast view of this cycle of life which ends with the ultimate impermanence, humans need to find purpose. What makes a person different from the rabbit, the hawk, and the osprey? Humans are aware of their immortality. Many spend their entire life searching for meaning in their existence. Often, they question what happens to them when they die. Some may conclude that there is only one way out of the downward spiral. They search for a way to accomplish immortality on their own. If they are unable to find a solution to their mortality, they may develop unhealthy behaviors. Men can learn to separate themselves from others. They develop the survival mentality that says, 'It is me versus them.'

"With this attitude, humans start to think that they are more deserving than others. They begin to compete for the pleasures in life. This competition leads to the illusion that the pleasurable things, the good and the fun things, are scarce in the world. This makes them compete even harder for ownership. To cope, men develop an image of the self. They place more value and importance on themselves than on others. Their self-aggrandizing thoughts spin out of control, and they adhere ever more strongly to the notion that they are superior to everyone else. Eventually they develop bad habits and personality traits such as intolerance, hatred, and prejudice."

At this point the hermit ran out of breath. He clasped his hands together in front of himself and gathered his remaining energy. "Inevitably, these people evolve full circle, become prejudiced, and then have difficulty getting along with each other."

"On this island, there are two mighty predators that rule the sky in summer, the osprey and the eagle. One has a white belly and the other has a black belly. To the rodent, rabbit, or snake, these two are equally feared and avoided at all cost."

The hermit was enjoying himself as he told this portion of the story. "The rabbit goes about living out his days feeding, reproducing, and dying. If he is able to avoid the large, white-bellied and black-bellied birds flying overhead, he will live another day. He is aware instinctively that they want him for an evening meal. The osprey and the eagle fly in the same skies, respect each other, and live out their lives much like the rabbits on the ground. The point is that the rabbit, the osprey, and the eagle live not independently of each other but interdependently. They exist together on this island and maintain the constant flux of life. They also maintain a balance. Unlike man, they rely on only instinct for survival. Man uses problem-solving and manipulation to control his environment.

"Sadly, away from this island world, men with white bellies and men with black bellies do not live interdependently but compete for the pleasures in their world and the respect of each other. They develop bad habits, start to hate each other, and become competitors against each other. However, in reality, the white-bellied man and the black-bellied man live in a world much like this island where there is an abundance of pleasures to be enjoyed. They could enjoy their finite lives so much more, like the osprey and the eagle, if they would not distrust each other—in other words, if they lived interdependently, and respectfully to each other."

At this point the hermit was exhausted, but he knew that his story was not complete. "Now, you have seen the polarity of the island in summer and winter. You have learned that there is a natural cycle of all living things. You see that all living creatures that are born must die. You have been told that all these living creatures live out their days interdependently to each other. You have also learned the exception is man. Remember that man seeks purpose and meaning in life. Man is aware of his own mortality. If he is unable to find a sense of self-worth, then he competes for the pleasures of life. He believes that these commodities are scarce. He sees himself as more deserving than others. He believes he is entitled to all his wants. He becomes wicked. He struggles in relationship with others."

He paused for several minutes. Slowly, the hermit smiled as if he had come to a conclusion to his dilemma. "Man has the ability to have creative and abstract thoughts. Through the power of reason and logic, he is able to ponder his origin. He yearns to know how and by whom he was created. With an imagination, man realizes that possibly a greater power than himself is responsible for his creation."

The hermit had concluded his story. There was only one question remaining. "This is the dilemma that faces man. If there exists a creator, then why does evil exist? Why is there disharmony in the world? Do any of the world's moral questions have reasonable explanations? Oh, how man struggles with his ever-spinning mind! He thinks about his origin. He seeks meaning in life. He discovers a hidden morality to all existence. He wonders about his own destiny. He has no problem asking the questions. He can determine a logical explanation for many of his dilemmas. His only struggle lies in the fact that he yearns to believe in something or trust in someone. Once that occurs, man becomes desperate to commit himself to a cause.

"It is as if a small computer chip has been deeply embedded into a man's heart. This chip contains the knowledge of creation, its origin, and an understanding of what is right and what is wrong. Most importantly, this chip reveals a glimpse of a destiny that says there is more to this earthly existence. The circuitry of this chip contains the possibility and the hope for a destiny beyond this life. There are those who contend that life is only an accident, and everything is a matter of chance; therefore, there is no purpose. This microchip says his belief is wrong. Man's heart says that all is not in vain. The world is not in chaos. The pounding of man's heart says the future is certain. The question for everyone is this: do you choose to listen to the microchip or not?"

The hermit was now yawning. "Come see me next summer, once you have gained more knowledge of diseases and more clarity of sufferings that await man along his path of life. We will then talk more about how to engage oneself in this experience of life. We will talk about the one greatest gift you have as a human being."

"What is it?" I was eager to hear more. I didn't want to stop here.

"If one tells you this secret now, there will be no more new seeds to plant next year. Nor will there be another piece of home cooked apple pie to eat next summer!" He paused for a second as if to consider the many options that lie before him in the moment. "Would you kindly, also, bring a copy of the book *Ordinary People as Monks and Mystics*? There are insights in this book that will be helpful to you on your journey of fulfillment."

With that thought, he bid me farewell. I was quickly off the island and thrown back into the contrasting world of medical school in the crowded inner city.

CHAPTER 9

The Encounter of Mortality

What a contrast the second semester of medical school was to the first. Last semester, we were introduced to the anatomy and physiology of the healthy, human body through which we came to appreciate its complexity and beauty. During the second semester, we revisited the organ systems, one by one, and learned the ways the body can experience pain caused by disease, illness, or trauma. The body can be destroyed in the blink of an eye or decline gradually over decades. Thousands of bacteria or viruses could attack an organ system, wreaking havoc on their normal state of functioning. A car accident could cause the driver to have permanent structural damage. Fine-conditioned legs that once had easily walked up a flight of stairs would now use braces or a walker to get around.

Individuals could expose themselves to environmental toxins . Even worse, one could elect to expose themselves excessively to habituating substances. Over time with chronic abuse, disease would occur. Chronic obstructive pulmonary disease (COPD), caused by the exposure to tobacco smoke, and liver cirrhosis caused by the exposure to alcohol serve as two well-known examples.

We were taught the presenting signs of many different illness. We were not yet learning treatments. We were told that it would take years to refine your expertise in diagnosis and treatment and become a skilled clinician.

Malaria was the one disease that intrigued me the most. Before arriving at medical school, I had spent all of my life on or near the shore. Most of my childhood was spent playing outside. Summers especially, I was exposed to evenings when the pesky mosquito would fly in from the marshes and become a nuisance. Often, the town would pay for a pickup truck to drive down the streets with a sprayer. The fumes emitted were supposed to kill the mosquitoes. As a young boy, I did not know that the most prevalent disease in the world was caused by a parasite living in those mosquitoes. Nor did I know that the parasite would attack red blood cells (RBC's) and cause these cells to swell with the excrement of the parasite. Ultimately, this would cause the cascade of fever, vomiting, diarrhea, sweating, seizures, and possibly death. Fortunately, antibiotics alter this cascade of misery. A kid had no way of knowing that the pickup with a sprayer that emitted a smelly cloud of fumes was so important. Looking back to my childhood, I now question whether it was wise to run behind the spray truck on these summer evenings and breathe in those fumes. I had no knowledge that malaria was only found in certain climates and rarely found anywhere near my hometown. I was never aware that it was likely that the exposure to those chemical fumes were more of a threat to my wellness than ever were a few pesky mosquitoes.

There are 69,823 codes in the International Classification of Disease (ICD-10). Many are rare and others common enough not to need the expertise of a physician. Other than illnesses, there are accidents; the resulting trauma can have you reporting to an emergency room unexpectedly. Your environment may also be a threat to your well-being. Exposures to excessive heat or cold can cause body systems to shut down. A casual hike during a vacation may turn into a catastrophic event if you are bitten by a venomous snake. Aging and its ailments are inevitable. In time, the hair will gray, the face will wrinkle, and the knees will weaken. Degenerative disease is unavoidable. So, as one can see, there are many aliments that can make you have a bad day!

Knowing all of this, there is a commonly occurring entity, an anticipated malady that occurs in the career of the medical student. It is a disease that can cause both fear and calamity. It is an illness that has its onset during the initial, intense review of pathology (the study of disease). Much like our childhood illnesses of measles or chicken pox, this medical students' disease will eventually invade most of its hosts. Until then, it hovers over each medical student much like the osprey along the shore that waits to dive down and attack its victim. Once the disease takes its course, the body develops an immunity. The student of pathology learns that most diseases will end with the suffix "-itis". This disease then would be called *iatrogenesitis* (in Greek this means "brought forth by the healer") The student realizes that with the presence of a multitude of possible medical ailments and diseases, he will likely come down with one. The student is vulnerable like the rat running along on the open sand with the eagle flying above, knowing that one day he will meet with his fate. With so much knowledge, so little experience, and absolutely no wisdom, the student concludes that he will come down with a terminal illness. The panic sets in. Most assuredly, he believes that he will be struck down by some itis, and his dream of becoming a physician will never become a reality. Granted, this sounds a bit theatrical. As in a Greek play, the main character is honorable but beholden to a tragic flaw. Nonetheless, this illness is real, and most students will be affected and have some degree of symptoms. Although the presentation of the illness can be severe, the survival rate is one hundred percent, and complications are rare.

It is likely that each physician has his own similar story from his training. For me, my encounter of mortality occurred while we were studying the heart and circulatory system. We were exploring the many arrhythmias (irregular heart rhythms) that the heart can encounter. Some were physiological, like bradycardia, a slow heart rate that well-conditioned athletes may have. Some arrhythmias, like ventricular tachycardia, can be lethal if they occur during a heart attack.

One afternoon in the middle of a discussion of arrhythmias, the professor asked for a volunteer to have an EKG run on them. In so doing, the professor could show the appearance of a normal heart rhythm tracing. An EKG is obtained by a machine that detects the electrical impulse that triggers the heart and conducts electrical impulses through special pathways that cause the heart to beat. By placing sensors, called electrodes, on various places of the chest wall of the patient, different configurations of these tracings can be obtained and recorded on paper. Customarily, twelve tracings are done, and the physician can obtain a vast amount of information regarding the heart.

Previously, the professor had shown us several abnormal heart tracings of arrhythmias associated with disease states. He advised us that toward the end of our fourth year we would take a full three-day course called advanced cardiac life support (ACLS). During this class we would learn to interpret the twelve tracings of the EKG.

Pridefully and knowing that I had been a well-conditioned athlete in high school, I volunteered to have an EKG run on my "normal" heart. The professor continued to explain the method of running an EKG, the correct placement of each lead, and then explained the need for shaving the sites where electrodes were placed. He then began to run the EKG and describe the normal EKG pattern. But once the tracing of my heart rhythm had been completed, he suddenly stopped talking and stared at the EKG tracing. Then he looked at me perplexed and asked if I was feeling OK.

In a masculine, self-convincing manner, I continued to lie on the exam table, "Oh sure, I feel just fine."

He continued to stare at the tracing and started to remove the electrodes from my shaved chest. "You can get up from the table now," he stammered. It was obvious that he was finding it difficult to find the right words to say to me.

Concerned, I asked if the tracing was normal.

"No. I need to speak with you after class," he replied. Abruptly, he asked for another volunteer to lie upon the table and have another EKG run. The lecture proceeded without any other interruption.

I do not remember much of the remainder of that class. At the end of the lecture I went back to the professor, and he advised me that I needed to make an appointment the following day with one of the cardiologists over in the university hospital. "You have a left bundle branch block. I'm not an MD but a PhD, and I have no clinical experience with the treatment of this irregular heart rhythm. You must see a cardiologist as soon as possible." I was aware that he would no longer look me in the eyes, and he appeared quite uncomfortable with the confrontation.

For hours that evening, back in my room, I studied EKG, arrhythmias, and bundle branch blocks. I learned that there are left and right bundle branch blocks. The bundle is the main tract of nerves which transverses the inside of the heart. It gets its impulse from the natural pacemaker, which is a group of specialized cells which are responsible for the automatic firing of the electrical charge which then conducts down the two bundle branches. One runs down the right side of the heart and the other to the left side. From each bundle, many small branches, like tentacles, protrude to the muscle cells of the heart. They are called Purkinje fibers. It's these nerves which contracts the muscles. As a result, blood is pumped to all the tissues of the body. I learned that this electrical activity is first detected when we are seven weeks old in utero. The bundle branches never stop conducting these electrical impulses until the day we die. Sometimes, it is possible to surgically implant a man-made pacemaker to stimulate the nerves and conduct electricity to contract the muscle. It needs not to be mentioned, but the bundle branches are vitally important to the survival of the individual!

I was sure the PhD said that I had a *left* bundle branch block. After hours of reading, I concluded that evening that the textbook did not give me a good prognosis. Left bundle branch blocks were associated with structural damage. The worst news was that they are associated with sudden death! What did this mean? Without warning, the heartbeat would suddenly stop! There was no way to determine when it might occur. Immediate surgical placement of an internal pacemaker was strongly recommended. The mortality rate was greater than fifty percent within five years.

This was likely the longest night of my young life. I don't remember falling asleep that night. Random thoughts entered my mind. "Would anyone miss me if I don't show up in class tomorrow? Who would find me if I suddenly died in the middle of the night? Maybe, I should clean up my room a bit! This would be a nice time to have a wife." This night, the textbook had not proved a good friend.

The next day in my morning classes, I was a wreck. Finally, afternoon arrived; I had a 2 pm appointment with a cardiologist. My head was hanging down. My perceived, sickened heart was pounding in my chest. The cardiologist stood over my EKG, and I anxiously awaited his interpretation. He looked up at me and saw the apparent gloom upon my face. "What did Dr. Thompson tell you about your tracing?"

"I have a bundle branch block. He asked me if I was feeling OK." I accepted the prognosis but could not hold back the quiver in my voice, "I heard him say it was a *left* bundle branch block."

The last thing that I wanted to see was a sad expression on Dr. Goldman's face. I kept my head down and struggled to continue. "I was awake most of the night reading about this condition."

Suddenly he interrupted me in the middle of my sentence. "Son, it is not a *left* bundle! It is without question an incomplete *right* bundle branch block. Why, ten percent of the people in this hospital have this condition, and it is extremely unlikely that *right* bundle branch block will ever cause you a problem."

He laughed and said that Dr. Thompson was wrong. "Those damn PhDs in the medical school don't know anything about clinical medicine. They have no idea how to treat patients." With that, Dr. Goldman stood up to leave. "I'll have to have a word with Dr. Thompson when I pass him in the halls this afternoon. Now, you don't worry, because you're going to be just fine."

With his parting words, I gave a huge sigh of relief and started to walk back to the classroom. One's first encounter with mortality can be quite alarming. It is amazing how quickly my emotions changed from fear to hope when I received the good news. I had learned an invaluable lesson this day. First, I will have my own patients one day. When I have to tell them the "bad news" that may change their lives forever, I will make sure my diagnosis is correct. If it's bad, I will choose to be respectful and kind to the recipient of the news.

The second lesson I learned this day is that there is a distinct difference between a PhD and MD. The PhD has a depth of knowledge in theory only, with little clinical expertise in the treatment of patients. The MD, in this case, a specialist in the heart, has a vast training and expertise in diagnosis and treatment of patients with heart abnormalities. I believed that one day, I would be treating patients and rendering compassionate medical care. I reassured myself, "After these four years of training, I *will* have the MD degree!"

CHAPTER 10

Living the Life of Self-Discovery

Summer break had finally arrived, and I had completed my first year of medical school. The first year had flown by. It was such an investment of time. I couldn't wait to go the movie theater, get a large bucket of buttered popcorn, and lose myself in fantasy. During the past year, everyday distractions like movies had not entered my mind. I was too focused to think about entertainment.

I gathered my books on anatomy, physiology, neuroanatomy, histology, and biochemistry and threw them into the trunk of my car. "I'm so excited! Summer break is about to begin. My brain needed a rest." During the drive back home, my mind wandered, and I began to think about my parents. I was looking forward to seeing them and sharing the summer with them.

I arrived home and promptly got into the daily routine. I usually got up late. I never had long to wait before my mom would serve up her delicious french toast with hot Aunt Jemima syrup on the side. My dad, having eaten earlier, would share the morning paper with me, "Son, here is the front section of the paper. I'm finished reading it. You know, you need to keep up with what's going on in the world."

I would respond, "Ok, but pass me the sports section." The only news of interest to me was there! Although it was a treat to sit and read it—I never had the luxury of such time while I was at school!

After doing her morning chores of washing clothes, dusting, and making the beds, my mom would settle down and watch her favorite show, *The Days of Our Lives*. I tried to join her, but I really never understood what all the excitement was about. "I started watching this show when you were in the 10th grade in high school. Something happens every day and I can't wait to see what will happen next," she would tell me as I sat there blankly staring into the tube. "Oh my! She's going to have a baby, and her husband had a vasectomy after her last baby a year ago!" At that point I was not sure that my mom even knew that I was on the sofa watching the show with her.

After dinner, we would all return to watching TV. It seemed like we all liked the same shows because there was never any arguing when *Gunsmoke* or *All in the Family* came on with a new episode. My dad always had to watch the evening news at 11 pm. Afterwards, we would change into our pajamas and wait to hear, "Here's Johnny." Then, we would settle down to have a laugh together while watching another run of *The Tonight Show* starring Johnny Carson. There was nothing better than watching TV and spending time with my parents and "Johnny."

I spent a lot of time with old high school friends. One day, several of us got together and drove to the beach. We had fun throwing the football around and laying in the sand. That evening we walked the boardwalk and watched the people go by. I had almost forgotten that French fries at the beach, heavily salted and sprinkled with malt vinegar, are the best pleasure food! When going to the beach, it was a "must" that I bring home a large box of caramel popcorn for my father to eat.

I enjoyed the days freedom given by the six weeks of summer break. Like anything that is pleasurable, they seemed to pass too quickly. One week before I had to return to school, I made the choice to drive back to the shore again and visit the hermit. The day was warm, and the sky was a cloudless blue. I took the long way around the island through the mud flats. The path was much easier today because the tide was extremely low due to a full moon.

In the early summer, the marsh was full of life. The fresh cord grass popped from the mulch of dead hay lying below. Insects like the no-see-ums, mosquitoes by the millions, and deer flies hovered in the evening skies. Most of the insects would be a food source for birds and marsh fish. At this time of year when the days are sunny, the fiddler crabs populated the mud banks and scampered about in the sunlight. There was music in the air that rang forth from the forest. The tree frogs, the crickets, and the many birds were singing loudly, as if to proclaim joyously the new births of the past several weeks. As I turned from the mud flats to the interior of the forest, I slipped and land on my hip and elbow. I was thankful that I saved the backpack full of the hermit's goodies from being crushed or getting soiled in the mud. I had brought him several packs of watermelon seeds, a bag of ground coffee, and the book he requested, *Ordinary People as Monks and Mystics*.

I entered the clearing in front of his home, but he was nowhere to be found. I heard a whistling sound nearby where his garden was planted. "Welcome back, old friend," he said while trimming his small tomato plants. "He who works his land will have abundant food, but he who chases fantasies lacks judgement. This chore must be completed, and afterward time will be made to visit."

Although he wore his straw hat during the summer, his face always looked like dark leather seasoned by the sun, wind, and salt. He finished his chores, and we walked back to the clearing, sat on a stump, and he handed me a drink of cool water. We sat there for over an hour and talked casually about my medical studies, his preparation of the season's crop, and the ways of nature.

"The no-see-ums are particularly bad today," I said. At the same time, I noticed that not once had he attempted to remove this annoying, biting insect from his exposed skin. He went into his hut and returned with a small jar of clear liquid, which he handed to me.

"Here, rub this on your exposed skin. This is a mixture of juices from mussels. They have an odor-emitting chemical in them which will deter the insects. If you lived here, you would notice that these tiny bugs never land on any mussels at low tide where the shells are opened or where one of the mollusks has died." He paused with a puzzled look on his face. "What is in these mussels that is so distasteful to these creatures? Sure is nice that it's there."

As always, our discussion eventually drifted toward more serious, thought-provoking topics. "You said on my last visit that you were going to share with me one of man's greatest gifts."

There was silence for several minutes as he prepared his words wisely, "Do you recall that there was a discussion about the struggles that all living creatures endure? Do you remember that there is impermanence, a birth and a death in life? Remember that man was unique? Man, with his power of discovery and self-recognition, was able to contemplate of his own existence. Being aware of death lead some men to believe of a greater power. For others, the thought of one's own death caused fear and confusion. This feeling separated him from the rest of nature's creatures. His anxiety made him think that resources are not abundant but scarce. Therefore, he was in competition, and danger lurked everywhere! To cope, he created illusions in his mind."

It was times like this, when the hermit got on a roll, that all you could do was listen closely and hope you would not forget one thought that was coming out of his mouth. I was mesmerized by his wisdom.

He continued, "There are three different ways for a disillusioned mind to choose to cope with the struggles in life. First, he may choose to be angry and attack those inconveniences that occur in his life. In so doing, he ensures that he stays in his own comfort zone. Another way of coping is to say what happens just happens, and you come to believe that you are helpless. You think you cannot change a thing. This human has a loss of heart. The third way of coping—an unusual one, yes—is for one to simply ignore the frustration and hurt in life and have the attitude of 'could not care less.' In so doing, this man shows resentment. He believes that the world is all messed up and the fault is not his.

"You asked about the greatest gift we have as a human being?' Well, simply put, it's free will, the ability to choose your path. You can choose one of these misguided paths; you can choose to attack, indulge, or ignore life's difficulties and the suffering in life. Or you can choose another path that can lead you to a life of joy and achievement and satisfaction. It's a path that can unlock a tremendous amount of fulfillment in your life."

The sun was beginning to set, and I could tell that the hermit was growing weary. He was quiet for a moment then smiled, "This conversation will be continued next time. Too much thought in one day makes the mind boggle. On your next visit, an exploration will be taken of a higher path that can be traveled."

With his parting words, I opened my backpack and handed him his gifts. He thanked me for the watermelon seeds and coffee. "Did you read the book *Ordinary People as Monks and Mystics*? The book describes ordinary people choosing solitary lifestyles so that they can inspire others to have healthier and more mature behavior. On page twenty-seven it characterizes one such mystic as living in silence and simplicity. He learns to listen to the world that surrounds him and begins to walk down a path of self-discovery. He avoids worldly distractions; he watches and listens to nature. His listening powers heighten, and he develops a keen awareness of himself interconnected with the living beings around him. Do you think a beach hermit can have these characteristics?"

"Yes, absolutely!"

He chuckled. "Farewell, my friend. When we next meet, bring along a book on the proverbs found in the Bible."

I started down the other side of the sand bank and turned to say goodbye, but he was gone. I imagined that he was off tending one of his garden plants or procuring clams for his evening meal. Whatever he was doing, I was certain that he was avoiding worldly distractions, watching and listening to the environment around him. Truly, he was living the life that was addressed in the book about monks and mystics. He was the one living the life of self-discovery.

CHAPTER 11

Shoes Under the Bed

The return to medical school was the time to become aware of yourself, your emotions, and your manner of expression. The study of the pure science such as pharmacology, pathology, and genetics continued, but the fascinating studies of psychology and the workings of the mind were introduced in the curriculum.

We began by studying the developmental patterns of normal growth and maturity. Psychiatric growth was the product of genetic makeup, environmental exposure, and social interaction with others. The basic premise was that as we mature, we develop a unique personality and form character traits. As a result we react to the fears, frustrations, and disappointments in everyday life. Similarly, we respond to the hopes, successes, and joys in our lives that also play a role in our development.

We learned about the theory proffered by Sigmund Freud and his contemporaries that involved the development of the mature individual and how he conformed to society. In this theory, the id, ego and super-ego related to the other. They support one another and attempted to balance the persona. When the three are working well together, the individual could thrive and adapt to their surroundings. Developing relationship with others and becoming dependent upon other persons could easily take place. The individual could actually thrive and be a integral part of society.

The ego, simply put, was a person's sense of self-esteem or self-importance. The id was a person's unconscious mind as it related to basic instinctual needs and desires. It could be remembered as the driving force that sought pleasure but avoided pain, at any cost. The super-ego could be thought of as that voice in the head that condemned your wrongdoing. It reflected social standards learned from parents. The super-ego was the moral authoritarian, the giver of punishment. It was the source of anxiety, guilt, or remorse. Once, a professor told us that the interaction of all these drives was like a bronco rider in a rodeo: the wild stallion bucking erratically is the id; the rider is the ego, pulling at the reigns and attempting to subdue and control the bucking horse; the thoughts controlling the rider and condemning him for being overly controlling is the super-ego. Without a doubt, there were times in my studies that felt as if I was riding a bucking bronco. There were times when I even felt like I fell off the horse.

Another area where we often stumble was how we respond to our desires. I remember the lecture on desires well, "The mature person not only has a code of conduct, but also has that voice that just says, 'No'. This voice enables us to live within the rules of society. This voice can be considered our inhibition." I remember thinking that this small word was quite important. I wished that it was not present at times, but without it the world would be in a state of chaos.

The professor continued, "It is the lack of inhibition that gets the maladjusted psychiatric patient in trouble with the world. It is this little voice that is in all of our heads that makes most of us socially appropriate and fit in just fine with everyone else. In psychiatric illness, the patient is unable to control the contentious drives between these voices. These patients lack inhibition and have no respect for the laws of society and the natural laws of living with others." He went on to say that psychiatry dealt with the abnormal behavioral patterns that people exhibit in society.

"I wish this professor could meet my friend the hermit." I thought. "I wonder, living alone in the world, would the hermit have to deal with abnormal behavior patterns? Maybe, that is why he lives alone? He gets away from everyone riding the bucking bronco." I had to get my mind off the hermit and back onto taking notes.

One of the more common abnormal psychological disorders was schizophrenia. The professor this day had another analogy that helped me remember this disorder, "Imagine a maladaptive individual who is always looking out of the window, and in his mind, he is somewhere else. Sometimes, even in his mind they are looking out of a window and there is no window in front of them." This was an interesting way to understand how a schizophrenic patient experienced the world.

The psychiatrist also explained the difference between the neurotic person and the psychotic individual, "When the neurotic looks at a refrigerator door that has a small black speck on it, he sees a spider. The psychotic individual, when he looks at the refrigerator and there is no black spot, sees a crawling eight-legged insect anyway and may even believe that it is possessed by demonic powers."

With an elementary working knowledge of the human mind, we second-year medical students began our rotation in psychiatry at Benjamin Bridgers Psychiatric Hospital. This hospital housed the criminally insane, as well as mentally ill patients who had failed to appropriately adjust to the outside world. For the patients' own benefit and safety, they could reside permanently in the institution. Many would remain there indefinitely since their families could not care for them. Therefore, they lived out their lives, confined within this institution, and became wards of the state. The rest of the functioning population never saw, heard, nor interacted with them. The only interaction these patients had was with fellow patients, the doctors and nurses who give care, and of course, the rotating second year medical students.

Undoubtedly, every physician has his own story about this journey and his first encounter with one of these individuals locked behind the doors of the psychiatric hospital for their own safety and that of society at large. My initiation into abnormal psychology was with a patient named Ramona Grace.

Each student was to conduct an in-depth interview with a patient. In so doing, we were expected to become comfortable speaking to patients and improve our communication skills with those who could not fit into society—in other words, to develop a rapport. We had to learn to be polite and professional. Prior to the interviewing sessions, the student was not made aware of the treatment nor the diagnosis of the patient. Hopefully, after this lengthy session, the student would also be able to determine the correct psychiatric diagnoses and would be graded accordingly.

The policy of the hospital dictated that the patient be constantly monitored by the guard outside of the room. For respect of the patient's confidentiality, the security personnel were unable to hear the details of the ongoing interview. Before the session occurred, in one of our classroom lectures, we were instructed to always keep ourselves between the patient and the door. The reason for this, as the professor advised, was that otherwise the patient could conceive of themselves as having the upper hand and being in a position of power. Feeling less inhibited, they would perceive that they could impede the escape of the caregiver. A loss of inhibition could cause the psychiatric patient to become more aggressive and possibly attack. Therefore, it was always essential to maintain the appearance that you, as the caregiver, were always in control of the activity and the topics of discussion.

We were also given a lecture on the art of communication and the use of open-ended questions to ease the flow of information from the patient. After the patient answered a specific question, the professor suggested that we ask one of the open-ended questions such as, "How does that make you feel?" Hopefully by doing so, the dialogue would continue, and the physician would gain more insight into the patient's problem. However, a one-hour lecture on the art of communication hardly makes one skilled in the intricacies of dealing with psychiatric patients. Like all clinical rotations, you were "thrown to the wolves" and learned by trial and error.

The day of my two-hour patient evaluation session arrived. So, there I was, alone with Ramona Grace in her locked room. Ramona Grace was a thirty-two-year-old, thin, well-built, attractive female. She spoke slowly and deliberately with a soft, low voice. She was pleasantly attired with make-up, some jewelry, and dressed in a tight-fitting sundress. She sat on the edge of the bed with her long, muscular legs dangling over the edge of the mattress. She seemed to squirm a bit during the interview but always appeared in control of her words as well as her body language. She smiled appropriately when I once interjected some humor. Humor, used in a professional manner, was recommended by our professors as a method to relieve tension and anxiety for the patient. I'll admit it did the same for me.

I asked her to tell me about her childhood. She warmly opened up and began to tell her story, "I was lonely as a young child because both of my parents had to work long hours. I had no siblings, and my grandparents lived many hours away. I grew up in the inner city and my parents did not allow me to go out and play unless they were at home and with me. Therefore, I spent most of my afternoons and early evenings in my bedroom alone. Because I spent so many hours alone, I developed a vivid imagination and even had an imaginary friend named Bobby." She struggled at this point. I underlined her next words because I believed that this was the first clue as to her deviant behavior. "We spent many hours together playing the childhood games that all children play."

Ramona seemed quite sad to me, perhaps a bit melancholy,

when she started recalling her relationship with her imaginary friend. I noticed that when she mentioned his name, she nervously but gently caressed her shoulder. This made the spaghetti strap to her brightly colored sundress fall off her shoulder. Considering her family circumstances, I thought that it may have been appropriate for her to have created this imaginary friend.

She paused for several minutes and seemed to be reliving some of those childhood fantasies alone in her bedroom with Bobby. It seemed to be an appropriate moment to introduce the open-ended question regarding her relational history. "How did it make you feel?" I asked. "You had an imaginary friend when you were young, but once you got older and developed real friendships did Bobby go away?"

Ramona Grace became even more dejected when she replied, "I had several attempts at long-term relationships, but they seemed to... just fail to develop lasting joy in my heart. So, Bobby was always there for me each time a relationship ended." She looked directly into my eyes, "But I am willing to try again. I feel confident with men, now. I believe that a lasting relationship may be in my future. All I have to do is find the right one."

The two hours it took to obtain all the patient's historical data went by quickly. Before I left the room, I scanned over my notes. I believed I had enough information to write a detailed report to hand in the following morning. I had concluded that Ramona Grace's diagnosis was that of a manic-depressive personality.

We were trained to close the interview with one more open-ended question to give the patient a chance to clarify any part of the preceding interview, "Is there anything else that you would like for me to know about you before I leave?"

Ramona Grace thought for a moment. While sitting on the edge of the bed, she arched her back slightly, opened her hands in a welcoming manner toward me, and kicked off one of her high-heeled shoes. The sound punctuated my attention, even catching the attention of the guard on the other side of the locked door. She said, "You, young man, can put your shoes under my bed anytime you want!"

I thanked her for her time, turned, and exited the room. "Taking off my shoes would be unprofessional. That just does not make sense. Why would I want to put my shoes under her bed?" I wondered.

The next day I turned in my seven-page report of the interview. I was pleased with our interaction, and I was convinced that I would get a good grade from the psychiatrist. After we handed in our reports, we were given an envelope that revealed the official diagnosis of the patient we had interviewed. To my surprise, I learned that Ramona Grace had the diagnosis of a maladaptive psychopathic personality. To my amazement the professor had underlined the correct diagnosis for me. Ramona Grace was a delusional nymphomaniac. Fortunately, at this young and tender stage of my career, I was not required to come up with the correct diagnosis nor was I responsible for the all-important psychiatric counseling and treatment plan of the patient. This would be left up to the experts in the field who had learned the true art and science of psychiatry.

For the neophyte, the second-year medical student, understanding the human mind was a fascinating journey. It could lead you down many different paths of the psyche. It took me several months on the psychiatric floor and numerous interviews with psychiatric patients to fully understand the proposition that Ramona Grace had made in my first psychiatric interview.

Being naive was not a maladaptive behavior or a defect in personality. It only meant that the conscientious medical student spent too many hours in the books and too few hours in the real world. Fortunately, once I finished my rotation in the psychiatric hospital, I was well versed in many of the calamities of the human mind. Most assuredly, upon my return to a medical hospital for the rest of my clinical rotations, and perhaps, even upon my return to the Friday evening visits to the Rosebud Tavern, I would not miss the subtle presentation of the arched back and high heeled shoes of my next encounter. However, one need not worry. *My shoes were staying under the bed that I chose: that twin bed on the second floor back in the home of Mabel Levine!*

CHAPTER 12

The lesson of the Three-legged Stool

In the blink of an eye, half of my medical school training was complete. The upcoming summer would likely be my last extended stay at home with my parents. Once we started our clinical rotations at the beginning of the third year, we stay at the hospital until we finish our training. Only an occasional long weekend would be granted at the end of a rotation. For that reason, I planned to spend as much time as possible with them. Being away at school for nine months at a time, I could appreciate the subtle changes that the passing of time and gradual aging could have on my parents. When you see someone daily, you don't notice this slow process of change. There were other things that changed as I parachuted in and out of their daily lives, like their interests and activities. When I was home more often, the events in my life were the center of their day to day living. Now that I was away most of the time, I was no longer the focus of attention. I could not be upset. This was just the way it should be.

They spent many years nurturing me and providing for me, and now they deserved a new life of their own. They had told me, when I first went away to college, that the transition had been difficult for them—the empty nest syndrome. To hold on to something or someone too long, especially when it's time for them to be free, could cause sadness. Unfortunately, change was difficult. I suspected that this could be eased by seeing this time as one of the many steps along the way to maturity.

For the two months of summer, I spent time with parents daily and slowed down the awareness of their growing old. Our relationship returned to the way it once was.

During these summer months, my parents did not worry about my well-being and enjoyed caring for me. My dad had always worried about his finances and was always concerned if he would have enough money to make ends meet. He worked hard all his life to make his family secure. I suspect, now that he had retired from working as a carpenter, he would be pleased that his son would not have those calloused hands that he once had. If only his arthritic fingers could talk, many a tale of hammers missing the nail and landing on the nails of fingers could be told.

I remember when I was eight years old, my father came to Thanksgiving dinner with a towel tied around his left hand. We were all concerned. My mom fetched a clean towel to wind around his hand to stop the bleeding. "George, what have you done to your hand this time? You know it's Thanksgiving, and you were supposed to get cleaned up before dinner."

My dad, slightly embarrassed, did not mince words, "The circular saw kicked back, and it struck my hand." After eating his pumpkin pie, he was the first to excuse himself, and off he went to his workshop. His hands were always bandaged and scarred from manual labor.

Those hands exemplified a work ethic that taught if you wanted to get the job done, then you worked hard, and you kept working until it was done right. Now after all those years, I wish I had told him what an impression he made on me that day. "Thanks Dad, I was watching."

Similarly, my mom worried constantly that my clothes were not clean and I was never eating right. She said I always looked too thin. Now, I regret that all those nightly home-cooked meals as a teenager had been taken for granted. However, after eating in a hospital cafeteria for nine months, that summer each supper was enjoyed and heartily praised. I also remember that my mom always kept the home neat, organized, and clean. This was certainly not the case for me back at school, living on my own in a single bedroom. Socks and underwear were thrown about my room. Out of habit on Friday evenings, just before going to the Rosebud Tavern, I would pick up all the empty potato chips bags and cola cans that had accumulated over the past week, straighten up the room, gather all the dirty clothes, and do a load of laundry. It was enjoyable to be home and not have to worry about these Friday night chores. Moms are the best!

I took a job as a first assistant to a group of surgeons at my hometown hospital. I was treated as if I was the hometown kid who had made it big. The nurses and hospital staff treated me with respect, but I really wanted to earn the respect of the general surgeon who stood across the operating table from me. During an operation, he expected me to perform at a high level. The learning curve was steep. The surgeons were demanding, but they taught me much about being a first assistant in surgery. As we talked about each case, the general surgeon would occasionally ask me questions about the anatomy he was repairing. Applying that knowledge on real patients was exciting. That summer, I logged more than three hundred major cases in the operating room and became quite proficient as a first assistant.

One surgeon, Dr. Graybar, was a tyrant who expected much from the team assisting him. He took me under his wing, and we quickly became the talk of the hospital because we worked so well together. The culmination of our summer together came in my last week of work. Dr Graybar was going for the record. He proudly called it his "PR" (personal record). With me as his first assistant and his girl Friday, Judy, as circulating nurse, we together performed an appendectomy from skin to skin in twenty-one minutes! This beat his previous record by a two-minute margin. We were all quite proud of our accomplishment.

To my surprise on our last day of work together, he asked me to come to his office at the end of the day. It was then that he gave me a crisp, new one-hundred-dollar bill. In his mind, he gave it to me because it had been earned, but in my heart, it was a gift of friendship and respect. It was my first earned income as a physician. It had been the best summer of my life up to that point. The days in the operating room quickly passed. That moment in the sun and being the recipient of so much attention was a huge morale booster.

Before the summer ended, there was only one duty left undone. I was eager to make my beach drive and visit the hermit. I deliberately waited until the last week of summer vacation. I wanted his wisdom to be fresh in my memory when I returned for the even more challenging third year at school. Again, I debated as to what I should take in my backpack as a gift to my scholarly friend. The purchase of the book was easy. He had requested a textbook by Salinger on the biblical proverbs. It was expensive, but I was able to find a used copy in a second-hand bookstore.

For his culinary enjoyment, I decided on my greatest challenge yet. My mom had just cooked one of her made-from-scratch strawberry shortcakes. The cool whip topping was placed in a small Tupperware bowl and put on ice in a small cooler along with the berries in a separate bowl. I planned to place the freshly cut, juicy berries on the cake and add the cool whip topping in front of his eyes. This would be performed as soon as I entered his retreat. His look of surprise and the sheer delight on his face would be worth all the effort.

I enjoyed my walk along the path from the south. I had spent most of my summer in an operating room, so being outside and walking through the maritime forest was delightful. As I entered the clearing, I found my friend sitting on a stump working on his fishing poles and lines. We greeted each other with handshakes and claps on the back. The satisfaction he took in eating the strawberry shortcake was pleasurable to both of us. It came off just as I had hoped.

Once he had finished his delicacy, we began to talk aimlessly about plants, flowers, and his neighbors: the animals. Sitting as usual on our respective stumps, he began extolling the virtues of a nearby colic root plant and its tiny white flowers that adorn the free-standing stalk, "They were plentiful this year. This was a good thing because at the base of the flower there is a bulb that has a sweet-smelling jelly material. Using beeswax and this jelly, one is able to make the bars of soap that are used to wash clothes."

He went on to tell me that the croaker was his favorite fish to eat because it was so easy to catch. "Two years ago, by trial and error, the croaker absolutely could not resist a bloodworm. When the bloodworm is impaled with a hook, and the line is weighted and left on the bottom of the canals in the marsh, catching every meal is there for the taking." He warned me, however, that the abundance of bloodworms and the spawning of the croaker only lasted for about a month in the summer.

As always, we eventually settled down to the deep, thought-provoking dialogue that I yearned to hear each time we met. "Last summer you said that you would share with me a path that I could choose that would unlock tremendous fulfillment in my life," I prompted.

He smiled with that familiar grin that I had come to anticipate. "Let us first review our journey up to this point. We said that in each life there is suffering. We seek pleasure and run from pain. We look around ourselves and realize that there is impermanence to all living things. We separate ourselves from the world, and we develop the attitude that resources are scarce. Then, we compete for them and develop the misconception that it's me versus them. In avoiding the suffering, we develop distorted attitudes. When we last met, you learned that you could stay in your comfort zone and just get mad, you could lose heart and feel helpless, or you could choose to care less and build up resentment."

He stood up and walked around a bit. I could tell that he was rehearsing his words silently before speaking out loud. He was finally going to give me the "gift" that he was leading up to over the past two years! He was standing directly in front of me and looking down at me. "Now, here is the choice, the choice that can give you tremendous fulfillment and joy in your life. Actually, there are three choices! The first is simply: work. What you choose to do in life gives you purpose."

I felt as if I was listening to an enthusiastic motivational speaker. I pleaded for him to continue. He said, "You must engage in the experience called life. To truly make a difference and have purpose you must get up from your seat! Be a doer and not just an observer. Be a participant and not a spectator! We are all made to work. It is said that whatever you do, do it with all your might. One may gaze upon the many animals of this marsh and see that each works to provide its own nourishment and shelter. The pelicans dive for fish. The ghost crabs find insects crawling about the sand and have a plentiful meal. Likewise, man must work to provide for himself. It has been said that if anyone will not work, neither shall he eat. We were created with two arms and two legs. Why do we have five fingers on each hand? Those ten fingers can create masterpieces and perform complex functions. We are physical beings. We were made to work."

At this point, the hermit went into his living quarters and came out with an object in his hand. He showed me a wooden stool that he had just finished carving, presented as if he were entering the stool into evidence in a trial. "How do you like the wooden stool? It's like the ones on family farms that young men use as they milk the cows. Notice that it has only three legs. A milking stool has only three legs and not four for a reason. Did you know that a three-legged seat is the most stable structure to sit upon? A four-legged stool must have equally cut legs, or the stool will not sit well on the floor. One would be constantly shifting if the legs were unevenly cut. Likewise, if the ground was uneven, then a four-legged stool would be constantly shifting. The same issues of balance do not plague the three-legged stool. It is the most stable and the easiest to build.

"Three legs; not two, not four, symbolize stability for stools and for life. It is good to have three pillars upon which to sit firmly when on uneven ground. Likewise, you cannot go wrong with three-point fixation when facing difficult challenges in life. For example, when climbing up and down a tree or ledge, it is safer to have three points of contact. It is not so smart to hang by one's hands only. So, it is the same with humans when they want to succeed. They are always most stable depending on three prongs, or legs for support. The fact that man has the desire and innate physical ability to do work, this is the first leg upon which he may find meaning. Man can find purpose in this life by working."

I momentarily interrupted, "Yes, I just learned that you use three-point fixation to reduce a fracture!"

The hermit continued quickly so that he would not lose his train of thought, "Now let us direct our attention to what the second leg of the stool represents. As you see, man stands out among all the creatures because of his unique ability to change the environment surrounding him. Doing so, he may live a little more comfortably. He does this through work with his physical body. Man also stands out because he has emotions. Man can respond to his environment with feelings. As you know, this can be beneficial or troublesome. Thus, the second leg to the three-legged stool is our ability to respond to our environment with our heart. Human emotions are innumerable and complex. Some of these feelings promote a state of wellbeing like joy, satisfaction, elation, and contentment. Other emotional states are negative and may be described as fear, guilt, and envy. Many people live out their days knowing that it's the relationships with others that make life meaningful. It is true that the many animals of the marsh mate and reproduce. It even seems, in some species, that a bond between the pair exists."

The hermit actually began to laugh out loud. "You should watch the horseshoe crabs as they mate in spring. Only when the moon is full and the tide is low do they come on shore. Among the thousands that arrive, each selects only one mate, and then the orgy begins. The female and the male attach to each other, and soon the incoming waves toss them about. There is an obvious attraction, but one would not consider that there is any emotion like we humans greatly enjoy."

The hermit became quiet and walked around in circles collecting his thoughts. He started again on a more serious note, "Of all the feelings we share with others, there is one that is the greatest. It is the single most important emotion. Having it is to have a meaningful experience in this life."

The hermit made a fist and pressed it to the middle of his chest. "It is love! You can be a great rhetorician, philosopher, or leader, but if you have not love, you become like a squawking sea gull. You could unravel all the mysteries of this marsh, but if you have not love, you have nothing. You could bestow all the rich foods from this place to others, but if you have not love, you will profit nothing."

It was really getting good! The hermit was filled with spirit, and his words were flowing. "What is this thing called love? It is easier to feel than to put into words. Love is like a long winter night in this bunker. It has been said that it is long suffering. Like the morning sun upon one's face, it is kind.

"There is no reason to envy, boast, or be prideful when one lives alone here on the marshlands. Here, there is no other person with whom to interact, most of the time. In the world, these feelings exist when dealing with others. Relationships can be enjoyable, or they can be challenging. The best way to experience these emotions is to have a deep love for others in your heart. If one becomes rude, or mean, or thinks bad thoughts when you are here alone, then no one will hear you. You cannot get depressed about petty things when you are alone. However, you can rejoice in what is present around you. This is like the way of love. Living this life on the marsh, day after day, year after year, one learns to bear all things. One endures. This is solitude. This is love. It will never let you down. Love is unconditional. One learns to live with faith that the next day will be just fine. One lives with the hope that any future hardship will be fleeting. But the greatest thing one lives with is *love*."

The hermit struggled for a moment, looking to choose his words with precision, "Love sets the tone for your life. Let your love be without hypocrisy. This means that the expression of your love must be sincere, without a selfish agenda. It should also cling inseparably to what is good, like a tendon binds to muscle. The love deep in your heart should viscerally repel what is evil. As if engaged in a lifelong war, one should take any action to eliminate bad behaviors or emotions. Love is tender and affectionate. Love shares all and gives comfort and strength. Love honors the other more than self and facilitates the other person's victory. Love is like the encouragement given even when the game is over and you lost. Love says 'thanks' and tells others they did a good job. Love listens and cautions from a tongue that can steer the boat in a wrong direction. Love has zeal and passion; it is not like the sloth in a tree. In service to others, love is like a servant. Love rejoices in hope. It endures in troubles. Love is contributing to the needy and showing hospitality to even a stranger."

The hermit stood up and held the stool by one of its legs, "Now, one must learn of the third leg of the stool. Something must balance out work and love to make our lives complete and meaningful. This leg is more difficult to fully comprehend, even to become aware of. It is most challenging to sustain. Without it, work and love have not a..." He paused a moment then concluded with a giggle, "...leg to stand on!'

I didn't have any idea what this leg could be. I took in all that he had said and still had no idea. What could the third leg be?

The hermit again entered his living quarters. Returning, he handed me a fibrous white chunk from a tree trunk. He called it the heart of the palm and told me to chew it. This heart of palm had the taste of a sweet combination of coconut and pineapple. It was quite refreshing! My mouth was half full when I responded to his last remarks. "I don't have any idea as to what the third leg could be. I see you here surrounded by all this beauty. I appreciate your total immersion in nature, and I am beginning to understand your relationship with the plants and animals here on the island. I can imagine after being here for so long, that you lose your self-image and become absorbed into the environment. I somewhat do the same back at school when I become immersed in the books and the hours of study. I get it. Work is the first leg. Love is the key emotion for the second leg."

"It is selflessness," he interjected, interrupting my words and my chewing. "Of the three legs, this one is the most difficult to completely grasp. Sadly, very few people ever discover it. Similarly, once found only few choose to own it. To intentionally become selfless requires a sacrifice of your own wants and desires. You no longer seek your own pleasures. You take joy in the fact that you have assisted others in finding their joy. Selflessness requires the desire to give rather than take. Is it hospitality? Sure, but it is more. It is not merely the giving of physical things; it is deeper. At the core of selflessness lies humility." The hermit poured some of the remaining juice from his glass onto the ground. "You want to be selfless? You desire to be a servant? You want to have a humble heart and inherit the earth? Then be like this juice. It always seeks the lowest point."

He took another bite of the heart of palm. "The major characteristic of selflessness is humility. If death to the self could be as perfect as this plant, then its blossom in the spring would be humility! The only ladder to peace of mind and honor among other men and animals is to have humility. The path to humility can only be traveled through selflessness. It has been said that nothing can be done through strife or vain glory. All can be done in humility. Humility is not thinking less of yourself; it is thinking of yourself less.

"Selflessness does not come easy; there is an evil force in the world. Some people call it man's sinful nature. Your mind tells you to protect the self. The heart says you deserve the best for yourself. American culture abides by the notion that one must always win. Being first is the only option; second place is simply the first loser and first forgotten. Pride owns the heart. So, it is easy to see that pride is the number one enemy of humility. The great preacher, Jonathan Edwards, said that pride is the worst of vipers that lives in the heart. John Stott believed that pride is the essence of all sin."

"It sounds so difficult to become selfless. Can anyone even reach this state? You seem to have come awfully close to having it here alone on this island. I can imagine that it would just about be impossible to have selflessness in the real world off this island. How could anyone accomplish this? Is anyone truly humble? I think I am understanding why it is so difficult to find meaning in life!"

Dear friend, you have been shown what is needed to have meaning and purpose in life. Yes, it is difficult. The three pillars that have been described are important. They are a path to a life with meaning. However, we have not talked about how one arrives at the point of achieving them. Be patient, when next we meet, we will speak about what one must do to get there."

With this oracle ending, he hung his head in exhaustion. "This way of life can be difficult to discover and understand. Finding

119

this harmony, this kingdom that exists around you, is easy when you remove yourself from the influences of the world. The waters of a river with no ripples make the mind content, aware and able to grasp the splendor of this chosen path. Living in a world where the river is turbulent, it is more difficult to find this path. This is the world to which you are about to return. One can choose to live in a river with no ripples, the world where hermits live. Some choose to jump out of the river, stand on the bank, and watch their lives pass them by without passion. They are observers only. Others choose to take the chance and jump into the wild river. These people work the rapids to their advantage, learn to help other struggling companions, and on many occasions become submerged under the water while keeping others afloat. These people are participants. They have found true meaning in life."

He thanked me for the scholarly textbook on Proverbs. He held the book for a moment then returned it to me. He advised me to be a lifelong student and come to learn the wisdom that can be found in the book of Proverbs. He also thanked me for the strawberry shortcake, "There must be a mansion in heaven that is full of your mother's strawberry shortcake, and there will be many standing in line to be blessed.

"Next time, we shall continue discussing the way one is able to sit firmly on the three legs of this milking stool. Fatigue has set in now and so you are bid goodbye."

He turned and walked to his home embedded in the sand dune. He opened the large door and just as he was about to enter, he turned and smiled. The setting sun was shining onto his face. The wrinkles about his face appeared to come alive and deepen as he spoke. "You are always welcome here. You are a dear friend. Bring a Bible with you when we next come together." With these parting words he closed his heavy door.

"Be selfless," I kept repeating, hoping that I would not forget it. I wanted to have the mantra at hand for my third year at school. Although the profound meaning may fade in time, I was hopeful that one day I would come to understand the true revelation of his life's journey. Hopefully the sharing of his journey may help me to share his wisdom with others.

As I drove back to the inner city and my home at the teaching hospital the next day, I thought, "Being selfless—it is all about losing the self in this world. You must forget the frustrating things in your life and become aware that we are all in this life together. We should help each other. Life is a journey. We have free will, and we can choose to share the world's abundant bounty. We can choose to flow down the river or stand on the banks. Flowing down river of life seems like the better option! Being a participant is the right choice; we are made to work. It is human to have emotion. Humility is the secret blessing." In this frame of mind, I was ready for the next challenging year of medical training.

As I parked the car on the street, in front of my second floor room at the home of Mabel Levine, I thought to myself, "Wow, I just had the most exciting and inspiring summer of my life! Can it get better than this?" I was soon to find out. Yes, it just keeps getting more intense!

CHAPTER 13

The Laying on of Hands

The second half of medical school was all about the short white coat with pockets full of note cards and reference books. It was considered prestigious to wear this coat of honor. It signified that you had obtained the pure knowledge of the science of medicine and now you were ready to "take it on the road" or in this case, down the hallways of the hospital floor to practice the art of medicine.

This coat of honor had an added distinction for me. In the middle of the summer I returned to the school to be fitted for the two white coats the school provided. I went to the hospital via the entrance next to the admissions department of the school. There, standing on the granite steps, was a younger looking man wearing a blue sport coat. I noticed that his eyes briefly followed a few fourth-year medical students as they briskly entered the hospital to begin their day. Most of these students never noticed the young man sitting there.

The air was full of the sounds of birds singing in the two rows of crepe myrtle trees that marked the entrance. As I walked by this young man, I slowed down and smiled. I had to tap him on the shoulder to get his attention. "Are you here for your first interview, or have you been called back from the waiting list for a second session?" I asked.

I should have known he was here for a call back interview since it was early July. The initial interviews are conducted in the early spring. By late May, most students have been notified of their acceptance in the first wave of inductees. If you are called back in July, it can only mean that you have been placed on the final reserve. I was well aware of these last-minute openings that could surprisingly occur.

Catching my error, I told him, "Hang in there, guy. I know it's tough to be where you are just now, especially seeing all these white coats walking past you. I have been in your shoes and know how it feels to be so close but not there yet. Stay determined, and good things can happen."

He looked at me with a gentle smile. "Thanks a lot. I needed some encouragement just now. Have a tip on how to get accepted?"

"Be willing to sit on these granite steps as long as it takes, and when you go inside, just be yourself."

I walked through the doors that lead to the administration offices. "I wonder if he has met up with the secretary, Paula Simpson? A chocolate chip cookie and a smile from her would help him about now." Ten minutes later, I was walking out of the hospital with a pair of short white coats under my arm. I wanted to put one on, but the appropriate day for that was still a month away.

Clinical rotations started in the first half of the third year. Students study pediatrics, hematology/oncology, cardiology, and urology, among other disciplines. Also, there are the surgical rotations, which each student must complete. Orthopedics was my favorite specialty. Perhaps, taking care of the fractured bones on this service reminded me of the time when I was ten years old, fell backwards off a pogo stick, and broke my forearm. The fracture required an eighty-mile trip to the closest city with an orthopedic surgeon. He had to perform the surgery needed to properly set my two broken forearm bones.

Although classroom presentations of medical illnesses continued in the mornings, the afternoons and evenings were full of patient visits. It was correct to say that you were intended to repeat the history and physical assessment hundreds of times on your many assigned patients. The history included the chief complaint and present illness. You were expected to include what events precipitated the illness and any activities that alleviated or worsened the symptoms. Then, a past medical history was taken, which described any medical illnesses, surgeries, allergies, or the often forgotten childhood diseases. The social/family history and sexual history was always entertaining to obtain.

Just in case the patient forgot some vital information, the astute medical student then conducted a review of systems. It was here that every organ system from the brain to the skin, from top to bottom, would have questions asked of it. A short review of occupational activity and environmental exposures including drug, alcohol, and tobacco use would be added.

After all this was recorded, then the student started the physical exam. Systematically from head to toe, every part of the anatomy was viewed, palpated, probed, percussed, and auscultated (listening to the chest and abdomen with a stethoscope). In the first month, this entire medical history and exam would take over an hour to complete on each patient. By the end of the fourth year, one could efficiently finish each patient encounter in thirty minutes. Once this ordeal was completed, the student was responsible for recording the findings as an 'H&P' (history and physical) and placing them in the patient chart.

In the evenings, you were expected to study the particular disease state that you evaluated that day with the patient. The next morning, the professor or residents would fire questions at you on the subject during rounds at 6:00 a.m. As a third-year medical student, you were at the bottom of the food chain when it came to making rounds on patients.

On the clinical floors of the hospital each morning, teams of six to eight white-coated young doctors moved in and out of patient rooms. If you stopped and listened to such a group, you would appreciate the organization, depth of knowledge, and obvious pecking order of the doctors involved in the discussions. Despite the challenges that confronted the medical student each morning, it was the afternoon workups with patients that were the greatest challenge. One of the first feats to overcome was the anxiety of the laying on of the hands, the touching of the patient. The human body could be a beautiful art form, magnificent in its delicate inner workings. On the other hand, disease, trauma, and aging could take a heavy toll and reduce a body and its parts to near nauseating outcomes. Fortunately, most physical assessments had normal findings and were consistent with age and sex. You were taught what was normal, as well as the many pathological states that could be present. The exam was left to the student to learn by repetitively undertaking the procedure. There were hundreds of seemingly simple exams that must be performed on each patient, and the nuance of each must be worked out by each new practicing doctor.

One of the more challenging isolated exams I remember performing routinely is the rectal exam. In the hands of the skilled physician this procedure can provide important information. Unfortunately, no one tells the student doctor how much K-Y jelly to use. At first, he uses a sparingly amount. After listening to the groans from his patient, the doctor adapts and performs the next several exams with an excessive amount of the friction eliminating lubricant. The patient experiences considerably less discomfort, however to his dismay, he sees the inexperienced practitioner slip on the floor as he approaches the head of the bed. Many a disjointed young doctor has returned from the adjoining patient bathroom with a hand full of paper towels. Cleaning up the excessive jelly from the floor, the patient's bed, and the lower half of his white coat is an embarrassing moment for all in the room.

Another thing unique to teaching hospitals and the use of its medical students relates to the very mundane issue of budgets. Like many institutions, the hospitals were on a budget, and when it was possible, they would buy products in bulk. These constantly used products were bought at significant savings, but sometimes the quality of the product was lacking. One such item was the non-sterile, vinyl exam glove used by the thousands by students doing exams or procedures that cause you to come into contact with bodily fluids. To attest to the number of exams performed, it was common to see several boxes of gloves on the counter in each patient room.

I can recall an incident that occurred to me on my urology rotation. The study of urology pertains to the body's organ system which eliminates products of metabolism and excretes fluids. In layman's terms, I am talking about the production and elimination of urine. In males, the urological problem is frequently that of obstruction and enlargement of the prostate. One of the key elements that the third-year student must learn in this rotation is the refinement of the skill and art of performing the prostate exam. Much needed information can be obtained by performing this exam when trying to diagnose urological disease. Volumes of information are written about the disease and the treatment of the prostate, but very little is written about the actual art of performing the exam of the prostate. In medical school, it is expected that a fourth-year student is supposed to enlighten you as to the proper technique and well-known pitfalls of the exam. If you have the misfortune of having a "not-so-interested in teaching" student as your instructing upperclassman, then you are unlikely to gain the knowledge required. In my case, the upperclassman said to me, "I am only here because it is required since I am going to be a neurosurgeon, and I am not interested in looking at urine all day long." The only one left to teach any skills on the service was the chief resident, and I was too far beneath him in the hierarchy for him to be interested in teaching the skill of prostate exams. So, the scenario played out, just me, the patient, and the box of economy exam gloves alone in the room. The patient asked the question, "Why?!" while I asked, "How?!"

There are many parts of the art of medicine that are never explicitly taught but must be learned by trial and error. Upperclassmen say that these trials are rites of passage. One such rite is the prostate exam. It is a lesson learned by making the error, only once. It becomes an ingrained memory. The lesson is simple. You put on an exam glove and examine it for any small holes before you do the exam! The moral of the story is simply, not all exam gloves are created equal. Small imperfections do exist. This defect is what it is. It is a small hole that allows stuff in!

The science of medicine is simply about learning how everything works together, or in the case of illness, how everything breaks down. It has its own challenges and takes years to comprehend. On the other hand, the laying on of hands is the beginning of the art of medicine. It can have its misadventures, but with time one can become accustomed to its beauty. Even masterpieces of art can lack perfection at their conception. Even mis-strokes of the brush can be a learning process. Likewise, after years of training in medicine, the final product is a clinician who not only knows how to diagnose illness but can administer treatment. When the young doctor learns to show compassion and actually cares for the well-being of his patient, only then is the training complete.

CHAPTER 14

The Gift

The summer between my third and fourth year of medical school was but one weeklong. Much had to be done in such a fleeting period. My mom washed my clothes and again fed me the most delicious down east-style, homecooked meals. My dad poked around the house fixing odds and ends. He was always good at keeping the "honey do" list as short as possible.

With eager anticipation, I looked forward to my yearly visit to the home of the hermit. I knew the path well by now, and I soon found myself entering his idyllic, natural home. As I entered the cleared quadrangle, I found him sitting on a stump mending some of his clothes. For the first time, the thought occurred to me that his face was showing more age. He spoke about the long winter. He said that a hurricane had come last fall and had destroyed much of his store of supplies. He showed me a wound on his leg that he had gotten during the storm. It appeared to be healing but with significant new growth of light pink tissue running several inches down the side of his left leg. He said that the strong winds caught the shelter's large door as he was entering his home and lacerated his leg. I assumed that it had initially been a very deep wound. He also looked as if he had lost ten to fifteen pounds. Despite the events of the hurricane and the severity of the winter, he had a smile on his face and seemed pleased to see me once again.

"The wound bled profusely for about two hours. Fortunately, there was one tea bag left from a gift in the storage area, and when you mix that with some ground up leaves from the Yarrow plant, you have the perfect anticoagulant. You know, it is believed that the Trojan war hero, Achilles, used the yarrow plant on his soldiers in battle to stop the bleeding of wounds. Once the wound was packed firmly, then elevated for the night, it was ready for my antiseptic ointment."

"So, what did you use, without having a pharmacy nearby to stop the wound from getting infected?"

I expected him to show me some concoction that he had made out of berries, oysters, and who knows what. "Why son, who needs a drug store when one has a storehouse of acceptable antimicrobials growing all around you! For years now, in the garden just over there, have been thyme and garlic, grown from gifts brought to me by other visitors. Both are wonderful for the seasoning of food, but they are also remarkably effective in the prevention of infections in wounds." The hermit loved to lower his voice to sound dramatic. "You see, the secret is this: you mix up the two in equal proportions in a liquid paste like slurry using apple cider. Then apply a thin layer on the wound daily. This has always prevented any skin wound from becoming infected. This formula kills staph or strep skin infections. It may even cover pseudomonas; however, that has never been authenticated. In the past, for minor wounds, the use of ground grapefruit seeds made an excellent antiseptic. Certain friends come by and bring grapefruit in the summer, and saving the seeds for the next year's cuts and scrapes is important.

"You may also find it interesting that the walls of the sea cucumber are quite effective in treating fungal infections. Being an islander and wearing one's rubber boots too much in the heat will cause problems with the toes. A lotion made from sea cucumber will prevent fungal infections of the feet. You can find these critters just below the water around pilings on the muddy side of the island in late spring. They have a chemical in high concentration called holothurian inside their tissue. Scientists use it experimentally on mice to halt tumor growth. See these lesions on these arms? Too much sun exposure causes them to appear. By applying sticky ointment made from the sea cucumber on to these growths, one can make them disappear. These skin lesions reoccur every summer, so every year you have to prepare a new concoction. It is not enjoyable to gather this little fellow. Did you know in China and the East Indies, that sea cumbers are collected, dried, and cooked with soy sauce and ginger as a delightful gourmet. It's called 'Trepang.' . They are quite slimy to work with, but they sure are worth the effort. They keep the toes looking healthy and without fungal disease and the arms without skin cancers."

For a moment, I imagined I was back in bacteriology classes during my second year of training. I thought to myself, how does this man know so much about medicine? Was he once a physician, or is he an autodidact, reading widely on various subjects? "How do you know that pseudomonas is an infection that is difficult to treat and often resistant to first line antibiotics?"

I was not sure that he heard me. He stared off over the swales to the south for what seemed like several minutes. "My friend, do you know what it means to be holy?" I realized that he avoided answering my confronting question and responded by asking me a quite off-the-subject question himself. I was confused but in silence I attempted to formulate an answer. Again, several minutes went by and he finally turned to face me. "It means that if you are holy, then you stand apart. You have asked a fair question. Being trained in such matters, why it's appropriate that you should ask this probing question. Do you think that your professors back at the medical school would laugh at you for using this remedy?"

"They would likely ask me what books I have been studying from over the summer." We both laughed, and soon we were rambling on about the smell of garlic on the breath and how it kept misquotes away. We talked about the other herbs in his garden, and I suddenly realized that he never really answered my "probing" question. Knowing that the hermit was always in control of his tongue, I gave him the honor of not asking my question directed to him again. It was quite likely that he knowingly evaded answering the question about his past and chose to abstain from revealing too much about himself. After all, the hermit always encouraged others and rarely turned discussion inward upon himself. He was very aware and sensitive about showing any self-pride. Some things are better left to one's imagination. However, in my mind, I believed that he was once a practicing physician and chose to leave that world for this life of selflessness, discipline, and discovery. But, why did he ask me that random question about being holy? The hermit was keenly aware of his capability directing a conversation in the direction of his choice. Without a doubt, again he is setting up a discussion to commence in the near future.

My time with the hermit always passed so quickly. He was always encouraging and in good spirit. As usual, we spent several hours getting him up to date on my studies and the happenings of the outside world. Then, abruptly, he said, "You must come and see the new path to this place. It has never been shown to you. It is the front door to the camp."

With that, the hermit led me to the left side entrance to his home. There, almost hidden from view was an opening to a narrow path that meandered around through a dense, thick growth of marsh oaks and yucca plants. We traversed a swallow between two sand dunes. The hermit and I both had to bend over and lean sideways much of the time since the path was only about five feet high and no more than two feet wide most of the way. I imagined that the hermit rarely used this path for his daily activities.

We now were somewhere behind the sand dune that his home occupied. Suddenly the narrow path stopped, and there in clear view was another pill box structure. The door to this abode was half the size of the entrance to the hermit's home. The hermit opened the door, entered the dark room, and lit a candle, which was sitting on a ledge within reach of the doorway. He motioned for me to enter. "This is what can be called a closet for it is here that items rarely used are stored. Only with an infrequent need will this structure be entered, and only a few select friends have seen inside."

The room was cool and musty. It appeared to be no more than fifteen feet in diameter. The sides of the room housed a collection of boxes and jars filled with a multitude of supplies that the hermit may eventually require for unusual daily circumstances.

"Some of these jars are full of materials I use for planting; some are the result of experimentation." Pointing to several jars on the floor to the left he remarked. "These containers hold the results of experiments using Spanish moss, or old man's beard, as it may be called. Herbalists use it as tea to relieve rheumatism." Then directing my sight to the right, he added, "These jars hold the dried fruits of the saw palmetto palm that are plentiful in the swales between the sand dunes. Indians once used these dark blue fruits to aid in digestion. They also used the inner root bark as a paste to relieve insect and snake bites. It was in this room that the antibiotics and antifungals that were shared with you were perfected. There can be many trials and misfortunes in this wilderness area. One always needs to be prepared for the next dagger nature throws at you. Some of these containers hold dangerous materials, and so they must remain here and not in the house."

The hermit directed my attention to the small table at one side of the room. I noticed several horseshoe crabs, syringes, and small medicine vials, like the ones I had seen in the hospital. In the vials was a blue colored liquid. He picked up one of the vials, "Here are the results of the most recent study performed in this room. Did you know that the horseshoe crab has blue blood? It has a copper-based pigment in it called hemocyanin. This blood can quickly detect bacterial endotoxins, form a clot around the foreign substance, and then remove it from circulation. This blood must be unique and special because the horseshoe crab was here before the dinosaurs, survived the ice ages and remains today essentially unchanged over billions of years! By injecting a syringe into the heart of the crab, one can draw of some of this blood. Many experiments are planned in the future using this valuable resource. Did you know that this fellow is more like a spider or scorpion than a crab? Now, follow me."

He led me down some steps at the side of the room, which led to a narrow corridor. The corridor extended about fifty feet! The floor and walls were cement and had been painted a military-green to seal the cement. "This room was once used to store ammunition, and this small corridor leads to the ocean side of the island where a World War II observation tower once stood. The tower has been torn down since the war ended."

"I have heard my father speak about the observation towers, but I never knew where they stood."

"We will climb up some steep stairs, through a well-like structure. There is a manhole cover over the opening. The thick shrubbery has been allowed to grow over the manhole cover so that it may remain concealed from any intruders."

So up we climbed the solidly built steps and proceeded out of the manhole. The wind had blown several inches of fresh sand on top of the manhole. Cautiously, he moved the loose grass and shrubs near the opening so not to damage their root systems. The natural camouflage would therefore remain intact. We both had to crawl on our hands and knees for some ten feet before entering an area with smaller, rolling sand dunes covered with sea oats and the occasional wild berry bushes. I could hear the breaking of the ocean's waves just over the high sand dune.

We proceeded directly toward the ocean and traversed the last remaining and tallest dune. This dune on the backside was very steep and proved difficult to traverse. "Do you need a hand, young man?" The hermit asked. "You have not had practice climbing these dunes from the backside. This is the trick to getting up to the top; watch this maneuver."

He began to walk across the dune at a forty five-degree angle, increasing the elevation of each step ever so slightly. How clever he was! I wondered if he had learned all his tricks of living on the island by trial and error, much like we as medical students do when we learn in the hospital. I imagined that he had once, early in his life as a hermit, attempted to climb straight up the sand dune as I had and struggled. I chuckled to myself and thought how everyone struggles early on as we travel our chosen paths.

"You have now been shown the front door. You are the honored friend. Now, you may use this entrance to my home if you wish. Do not show it to anyone for this closet stores many important supplies that provide me comfort in this life."

I was honored and pleased to know that he considered me such a friend. The breaking waves could be heard crashing only some thirty yards in front of us. We walked down to the ocean, sat upon the flat sand, and peered out at the ocean.

"We should speak about gifts today. On each visit you bring gifts. Today you brought fresh oranges and a bag of pistachio nuts, and as always you brought a book that was chosen. Today, you brought the NIV translation of the Bible.

"This is a gift for everyone. We are all given many gifts, each one of us. People call these gifts their talents. Some are given many gifts, and some are given only a few, but everyone gets something. Some get the gift of swift legs and use their talent to win foot races. Others receive the gift of a beautiful voice and use their talent to sing to large crowds of people. There are a special, chosen few like the prophet Mohammad and the Buddha who have great gifts of insight and awareness. Many people, for thousands of years, have followed their teachings. But there was one special person, who walked on this earth and was given incredibly special, unimaginable gifts. He was a teacher as well. And people for thousands of years have followed him to the truth. For the past several years, my journey on this island has been one of spiritual discovery, as well. Thank you for giving this book as a gift today."

The hermit began to roll his finger through the pages of the Bible in his hand. "You know, even if you have read parts of this book before, one must read it over and over, each time as if it was the first. One needs to test what it says, wrestle with its meaning, and come to an understanding that makes sense for you. At times it is easy to comprehend; however, after studying for a while you realize that it takes a lifetime to take it all in and make it work in your life. The message here is timeless. It's like a light from a lamp that shines at your footsteps and shows you your way."

I thought for a moment, having some difficultly formulating my reply, "When I was living at home during my childhood, I regularly attended church and youth group on Sunday evenings. I was brought up in the church from a young age, but to be honest, I attended church and went through the motions but never really took in or understood the importance of all the terminology like salvation by faith, or sanctification, or even repentance. I wish I understood this gospel better and why it is so important. Being completely honest, I am not sure that this gospel is for me. Now that I am in medical school, I am convinced that I can accomplish just about anything on my own ability. I can pretty much control my own future. More than ever, I feel like I am in control of my destiny. I am probably therefore very much like you, in total self-control of my own world."

"Oh, if it were not so late! You have so much to learn! You have a misconception of life here on this island." He calmed himself a bit and changed the subject. "For you to understand this gospel would take many hours, and even then we would only have scratched the surface. Does it have answers that will help with your life here on earth? There are many devoted followers that say absolutely yes!"

It was the most impassioned and determined I had ever heard him speak. "There are many components of the gospel. For now, let us say that it's about faith, repentance, sin, assurance, hope, and obedience."

I was spellbound by his testimony. "Oh, without being remiss, one must also say it's all about following a man who lived an exemplary life of service to others. Faith is believing in something that you cannot see or touch. This book says that faith is the assurance of something you have hoped for, that is in fact true. Faith in someone or something greater than yourself will show the way to eternal life.

"Repentance and sin go somewhat hand in hand. Repentance is the conscious turning away from evil and making a complete change in life. By evil, I mean any harmful act of defiance or thought against another person or God. People call this sin. These unkind acts always cause collateral damage to those closest to us. There are consequences to every wrongdoing.

"Despite all the wrong things we all do each day, there is hope. It is called forgiveness. It is a big part of the gospel. Did you know that you are forgiven out of love and it is a gift? Once you know that you have been forgiven, you will realize that you are not alone. Then, you know that you are loved by someone. This can be quite perplexing."

The hermit stood up and stretched his legs. "So, you see my son, it's somewhat like one of those chemical pathways you studied in physiology your first year of study. Remember how each step along the way was dependent upon its predecessor and the final product came into being only when the chain of events had occurred? Likewise, an understanding of life begins an awareness that you are totally sinful and in need of forgiveness. Sincerely from the heart, you repent and ask for atonement, payment for your transgression. Then by faith alone, you believe that God will do what He says He will do. You put total trust in God and live in belief that He is in control of everything. You live the rest of your life constantly renewing your belief. The consequence of all this is a life of obedience, a humble servant heart, and helping others to get on to the same pathway. You got all this, right?"

He laughed boisterously and helped me to stand up. Then, pointing his index finger into my sternum he said, "Now, here is your homework. For the rest of your life, you need to let into your heart the one person in the world who can save you from your sins. He desires you and wants you to follow Him on this narrow, less traveled path.

"It is a shame that you did not carry a pen and note pad to write down this chemical formula for future reference!" We both started to walk down the beach. "Hopefully, one day you will find knowledge from this book. You know, there is something to believe in that is greater than yourself! You should not be afraid to explore all the ancient world religions. You must compare them and see which can add insight and strength while walking along your spiritual path. Everyone should find one's spiritual way in life. Without it, you are lost, and life will have no meaning. There is truth in this book, the Bible. It may take most of your lifetime to..." He took a deep breath, "...get it."

I could tell he was exhausted. "You have the free will to choose what you want to believe. Choose wisely; your decision will have everlasting consequences."

With these parting words, he led me down the shoreline toward my home. "These waves have never stopped breaking and washing up upon the shore. They will continue to do so indefinitely. Even your death cannot stop them. One day, a day of your choosing, you may want to read the stories in this book and decide for yourself if its truths can be of importance to your life."

At this moment, I placed my hand on his shoulder. It felt boney and small. "You promised to share the 'what' or the 'way' to achieve the selflessness that you described to me last summer. Just what do I have to do to be selfless?"

He grasped my hand firmly. "You are correct. We did agree to continue the discussion about selflessness." The hermit pointed three fingers in the air and shook them directly in front of my face, "Remember like the three legs of a stool, three pillars of truth are critical if you are to find meaning in life. There is work for the physical body to perform, and emotions will fulfill the spirit, love being the greatest. Then, to compliment and completely stabilize the first two, there is selflessness. There is a final message that you must hear if you are to complete the structure." He lowered his head. "This is not the correct time to complete our journey together. You have one more year of school to finish first. One must describe the gate to the narrow path, which is the way of selflessness, only when you have completed your time of formal training. The wisdom of this passage will have more value to you when you have the MD behind your name."

I did not fully understand his secrecy, but I did appreciate his hesitation since the day was getting late. I could imagine that it would take some time to share this final testament with me. I wanted the time to ask questions and come to an understanding of this important truth. There were many unanswered questions that had been raised today. I would eagerly await my next visit with the wise man. The hermit was right again: timing is everything.

After sharing this advice, he quickly returned to his sheltered world, and I returned to the busy world of a fourth-year medical student. My life was all about the discovery of medicine. His life was all about his work, his love, and his selflessness.

CHAPTER 15

It's OK to Let Go

The classroom activities were considerably reduced during the fourth year in favor of greater focus on patient care. History taking, physical exams, and the laying on of hands seemed second nature. The short white coat that had been proudly worn for the past year was becoming slightly disheveled. The pockets were loaded with reference booklets, index cards with patient reference numbers, and notes of wisdom from previous patient encounters. You think you have seen and touched it all.

The other enjoyable thing about being a senior was that you were no longer at the bottom of the status chain. When making rounds, you were still drilled with questions from a resident or attending physician regarding patient care, but now, once you responded appropriately, someone would show off their superiority by asking the lowly third year student a belittling and beguiling question. This quickly turned the attention from you to them. It was a relief not being at the bottom any longer.

As a fourth-year student, you were aware that it was your responsibility to teach the third-year student much of what you had learned the year before. A code of honor existed between the different levels of training; what knowledge you imparted had to be accurate. Day by day, and round by round, the pearls of medical knowledge were handed down to each generation. There was a saying that circulated around the teaching hospital, "See one, do one, teach one." It went without further discussion that with each "doing" a patient was being touched, poked, stuck, and even cut open. Is it not more advantageous to be on the sticking side of the bed than on the stuck side of the bed?

A special event is held during the second half of the fourth year. If you were approved by your resident, you could elect to take a rotation called the SAI, which means "senior acting intern." It was during this rotation that you provided the treatment for a patient without the direct supervision of a higher-ranking physician. I elected to take my SAI as the last rotation of my formal training. The first half of the rotation occurred at a community hospital two hundred miles away. My tour of duty was in an emergency department where I would treat and stabilize trauma patients. One of my goals was to learn how to perform wound closure by applying sutures to a traumatic cut on the skin. I was told that rural community hospitals can have a high number of trauma cases. Accidents occurred or tempers flared resulting in a visit to the local emergency room. Knife wounds were not uncommon. To get the best exposure, I would report to duty around eight PM and plan to spend the evening and the early morning hours in the ED. This decision proved to live up to expectations.

One particular late Saturday night in the emergency room proved to be an outstanding learning opportunity. The attending ED physician, Dr. Britt, had rapidly triaged and treated the seriously ill or wounded for most of the night. He worked without a break for six hours. Side by side, we rendered treatment and responded to any of the needs of our patients. Finally, things started to slow down, and we sat down to complete the medical records.

Dr. Britt looked up and said, "Nothing good ever happens after midnight. If you are outside of your house, and it's two AM, then you are about to give someone else trouble or you yourself are about to get in trouble. That trouble ends up coming into my emergency room and giving me a lot of work to do."

He gulped down a large cup of coffee and stood up from his desk. "Follow me, and I will show you what I mean." Together, we walked into the exam room. The ED doctor proceeded to describe how several men had been at a bar and had a little too much to drink. An argument between two of the men became heated and one took a punch to the face. He was in room four waiting to be rolled into radiology for a CT scan. The man in room seven, who had thrown the punch, got into a wrestling match on the floor with the other, and eventually lost the fight.

Dr. Britt pulled the sheet down away from the exposed back of the patient. There, in front of me was the longest wound I had ever seen. "We have here a twenty-six-year-old male with an alcohol level of two hundred and twenty who sustained a deep, sixty-eight-centimeter laceration to his upper back. Note that his subcutaneous tissue and muscle fascia are exposed. The laceration is deep into the first layer of both the rhomboid muscle and latissimus dorsi muscle on the left."

All this simply meant that this man had just met up with a very disgruntled opponent. This irate individual had literally "filleted" his back. At this point in my early career, the suture ligation of this wound required a skill level that far exceeded mine. "The closure of this cut is out of my pay scale!" I said. I had closed several small wounds to arms and legs earlier in the evening. Dr. Britt had even remarked that I had performed an excellent closure, and he was one doctor who didn't have the time to give empty compliments. Throughout the evening, he suggested several advanced techniques and showed me "the horizontal mattress" stitch for the ligation of a corner of a wound. I was excited. I knew I was improving as the evening progressed into the early morning.

Yet here we stood looking at this patient with a laceration all the way across his back. Dr. Britt thought for a moment and walked out of the surgical room. He looked down the hallway of this busy ED. There were as many patients in treatment rooms as the waiting room. When he came back he said, "Irrigate the wound well and remove any foreign bodies such as dirt or cloth fibers. You will have to do a layered closure. First, cover the exposed muscle with the fascia tissue that encapsulates the muscle using absorbable sutures. Come get me so that I can see your work and approve the closure of this important layer. Then, you may proceed with a primary suture ligation of the skin. I will ultimately be responsible for the procedure. So, do a good job!" With that he walked out of the room.

Without hesitation but with some trepidation, I began the ninety-minute challenge of putting this man back together. After covering the muscles, Dr. Britt inspected my work, seemed satisfied, and advised me to complete the procedure. When finished, I had placed one hundred and twenty-six sutures in the closure of this wound. Dr. Britt then told me how he wanted the wound dressing applied. He went into great detail about what the patient must do daily as wound care. "You may want to write this all down and hand the wound care instructions to his girlfriend who is sitting in the lobby. Before you let him leave, recheck his alcohol level, and document in the medical record that he was able to eat, urinate, and walk down the hall on his own. He still is in no condition to do any of these things."

"He sure is going to have a huge headache in the morning."

"He's going to have intense pain in his back, too. Give his girlfriend two pain pills to administer when he sobers up." That was a good idea. I had forgotten about pain medication. "It's easy for you young doctors to get all caught up in the procedures and forget about follow up care."

I wanted to thank Dr. Britt for allowing me to do the closure, but he was called to another exam room before I had the chance.

Dr. Britt was a great doctor. He was on top of every detail, worked non-stop, and responded compassionately to the needs of each patient. He was truly exemplary.

It is the little things that you remember the longest. Granted, the ninety minutes spent performing a procedure were worthy, but what Dr. Britt said to me later has lasted a lifetime. He returned as I was finishing up the dressing. He only stayed for a second.

"Well done, Dr. Carpenter," he said.

This was only one of the presentations that morning and this just one shift of many over the six-week rotation. This patient stood out. I was paired with an amazing ED physician that morning who not only had great skills but also great confidence in my ability. Although his department was in near chaos, he always seemed in control of each and every emergency. I remember as I was leaving, I did thank him for giving me the opportunity to help him care for his patients. I thanked him especially for giving me the confidence to do the job. I will never forget what he said to me that morning. He smiled and gave me one more pearl of wisdom.

"Charles, never let them see you sweat."

It may be true for the public that if you are out and about town after two am, only bad things can happen to you, but it was not so for the medical student. Countless medical students have fine-tuned their skills in the early morning hours in a busy emergency department. These hours seemed to go by quickly, especially when your rotation found you in the surgical suite of an emergency room. Perfecting a surgical skill could be one of the most exciting times in the young career of a developing clinician.

Often, I have wondered if community emergency rooms were not over utilized and their attending ED doctors not stressed and over worked, then would Dr. Britt have given me the opportunity to perform those skills that night? Likely, he was just trying to get through another shift, and I was a resource he could use to alleviate some of the work that had to be done.

It is unfortunate that people make poor choices, must suffer, and spend their nights in an emergency room. Why do people have accidents and suffer so much? I can think of two reasons. First, bad things happen because there are lessons that the recipients must learn. The other reason is the silver lining for the medical student. He is able to perfect his skills and gain confidence.

The second half of my SAI rotation found me at a regional burn unit. There are moments in your life that you never forget, and they become a part of your character forever. One of these life-defining moments occurred while I was in this burn unit.

The skin on our bodies is mostly taken for granted. During our lives, it protects us from our environment. We are exposed to millions of microscopic bacteria, viruses, and parasites that literally want to eat away at our skin. Daily it rejects harmful organisms from invading deep under the skin and causing damage to other organ systems. When the skin is traumatized, like a superficial burn, it repairs itself quickly. First degree burns, like a sunburn, peel away without any scarring. Second degree burns will heal in several weeks but can cause a lot of pain and will leave some scarring. Third- and fourth-degree burns penetrate more deeply and cause permanent damage to the underlying structures such as tendon and bone. Nerve endings in the skin are lost, resulting in loss of the sensation of touch forever.

While working as a SAI intern in this burn unit, a call came in over the paramedic radio and announced there had been a car accident. The automobile had caught on fire and an eighteen-year-old female had been saved from the flames. The paramedic on the radio stated that patient was in route. Her ETA was three minutes. Personnel in the ambulance had started two IV's; fluid resuscitation was important since traumatized skin loses large amounts of circulating fluids. I was assigned to render her continuous care. She arrived with wet dressings about her anterior chest, left arm, and her entire face. Her blonde hair had been mostly singed, and her right hand, for some reason, was spared from injury. She rolled into my exam room and the curtain was pulled closed for privacy.

The chief trauma resident assigned to the unit rapidly assessed her wounds, then turned to me. Sternly and confidently, he advised, "You need to maintain the IV fluids. Watch her airway. At this point she appears to be oxygenating adequately. She may need a surgical procedure, the cricothyroidotomy, if she has an obstructed airway. Make an incision through the skin and cricothyroid membrane to establish a patent airway. This is only done in a life-threatening situation, such as with this case of massive facial trauma. If she drops her oxygen saturation, then do this procedure quickly! With the amount of trauma to her face, thorax, and extremities, as well as the possibility of internal abdominal injury, I will give her the white tag."

I was writing down all the instructions as quickly as I could. "Give her some pain meds, doctor. I will call the attending trauma surgeon and see how aggressive he wants to be. Three other victims from a house fire have just come into the unit. My first-year resident informed me that they are all red tags, so I am going to leave you with this girl. I will be down the hall. I will return and let you know what the attending surgeon decides about this patient. You call for me if you need me."

As part of the orientation to a trauma rotation, all the medical students are required to take a ten-hour course called Advanced Trauma Life Support. It is in this course that you learn that triage is a system of sorting and prioritizing victims of trauma based on the situation and available resources. Triage and the use of color tags is used to establish order and provide the greatest good to the greatest number of people. Usually the colored tag is attached in an easily visible location on the patient.

The red tag represents "immediate" need. This victim requires attention within minutes to one hour from arrival to avoid death or major disability.

The victim who is given the green tag is designated "delayed." These individuals have wounds that can wait one or two hours for definitive treatment. The delay in time will not endanger life or limb. These patients may have fractures, superficial lacerations, or minor burns.

The white-tagged trauma victim represents a group called "expectant." This group of patients has injuries that overwhelm current resources. These victims have injuries that allow for a slim chance for recovery or survival, but with excellent medical care have an opportunity to survive. (Opportunity is what the physician wants to give each patient.) Only when resources are available should stabilizing procedures be given to these victims. Otherwise, one only provides medication that will minimize the pain.

The black tag is used on victims who are lifeless or have sustained injuries that are not compatible with life. If the patient was responsive to painful stimuli, the only humane thing to do was to give a shot of morphine and alleviate the suffering.

Having established that my patient was a white tag, I began my assessment. She was alert and moaning as if in fear. I introduced myself and proceeded to unveil her arm and chest from the wet sterile dressing covering her burns. The burns to her chest and left arm were a mixture of mostly second and a some third-degree burns. I then removed the wet cloth from her face. Her lips were essentially gone. She was breathing from contracted muscles around the mouth which exposed her blackened teeth. Her eyes were effectively also gone. Only the socket with some charred debris remained. The bone of her cheek and brow was exposed, and blanched bone was apparent. She was awake and alert but unable to speak. I was amazed by her calmness as I sat down beside her. I held her unharmed right hand. I asked if she could feel the clasp of my hand around her right hand and if so, she was to squeeze once. She squeezed once. I instructed her to squeeze my hand once for an affirmative answer or twice for negative.

For some time, we spoke in this manner. I tried to give her words of encouragement. I asked if she was comfortable...one squeeze. I asked if there was pain, and she responded with one squeeze, then two squeezes. I then asked if she knew that things looked bad for her, and she immediately replied with a no (two squeezes). Several seconds later she responded with a slow yes (one squeeze). I asked if she was a spiritual or religious person... one squeeze. I asked if she was a Christian...one squeeze. Without reservation and as gently as I could, I asked if she was prepared for a bad outcome... one squeeze. I noticed that the tears that had been welling up in my eyes and had dropped off my cheek and onto her hand. It was then that she grasped my hand four or five times in succession. She held firmly as if to say, "It's OK...I'm OK." She held my hand for several minutes as tightly as she could. I noticed that her squeeze was getting weaker. I remember asking if she had family nearby. She gently squeezed yes. Then, without even thinking of her response, I asked, "You do know it's OK for you to go now if you want?" She responded with her final...yes. Her head turned slightly as if she were looking straight at me before she took her last gasping breath. She squeezed my hand firmly and died.

I sat there staring at her charred face, imagining what she may have looked like just minutes before. Since she was blonde, I imagined that she once had bright blue eyes. I hoped that somewhere, someone loved her for the person that she was.

The curtain suddenly flung open, a team of residents pronounced themselves, and asked what I was doing, "Why have you not given any pain meds or antibiotics?" The senior residents appeared frustrated and upset that I had not attempted to render treatment during the time that I had been with this patient. They said that I could get reported to the attending staff for lack of care. "Why have you not called for help if you were not sure of the dosages?" The two residents assured me that they were going to speak with the physician in charge about my apparent choking on the job and poor judgment.

I stood up, looked them squarely in the eyes, and spoke clearly and with firm conviction. "Do what you must. I feel good about the treatment that I gave this girl. I gave her what she needed. I did render care in the last moments of life to a dying person. In your eyes it may appear as poor judgment. In her eyes, she saw my compassion. That was what she needed the most. She needed to be touched. She needed to know that someone cared about her just the way she was."

These were bold statements. I knew there could be repercussions. These words addressed to my superiors were like adding fuel to the fire. To these residents, my apparent lack of caring for the patient was directly related to the adverse outcome. I started to walk out of the exam room. I had no regrets for what had just happened. "On one of my visits home, a wise man told me a truth that I now believe whole-heartedly." I knew in my heart that these residents may not comprehend what I was about to say. Most likely, they would become more agitated, more prone to report me. "I hope that you learn one day that it's OK to have emotions and share your love. Caring is part of our job."

There was no further discussion regarding this case from either the resident staff or the attending team of the burn unit. As I drove home, a warm and encouraging thought came to my mind, "Every young doctor needs a hermit for a friend!"

CHAPTER 16

Graduation Day

The day of graduation was a beautifully warm, sunny day. Many members of my immediate family were present, including my parents, my sister, her husband, and my two nephews. They had spent the night in a nearby motel. After breakfast, we all sat around the pool. My nephews and I jumped in the water, threw the football around to each other, and dove off the diving board. It had been a long time since my two nephews and I had played together. They seemed to have grown up quickly during the time I was away. They were both now in high school and starting to plan their own careers. Soon, the hour had come for all to get prepared and get dressed for commencement.

The event was held in the quadrangle of the university, just in front of the campus chapel. The area was about the size of three football fields end to end. The entire area was surrounded by large stone buildings, which housed classrooms and the offices of the university professors. A wide walkway outlined the grassy central area, and majestic, tall shade trees full of new spring foliage encircled the quadrangle. This day, several thousand chairs were placed in rows on either side in front of the lofty chapel and a stage set up at the head of the rows. Hundreds of family and friends stood under the shade of the trees, using their programs to fan themselves in the heat. Others braved the hot sun and brought folding chairs to sit behind the faculty and graduates in the center of the quadrangle.

A center aisle had been roped off and remained open down the entire length of the quadrangle. At the opposite end of the chapel stood the student union building. Inside the graduates made their last-minute preparations and proceeded to place themselves in the exact order in which they would be seated and called onto stage for their diploma. Literally, the stage was set. Everyone outside was anxiously awaiting the start of the ceremony.

The ringing of the bells high above at twelve noon announced the opening of the affair. To the left of the stage, the university band started playing the school song. With much pomp and circumstance the ceremonial officials, led by the president and vice presidents of the university, exited the chapel, walked on stage, and sat in their appointed armed and cushioned wooden seats. Each college of the university that was honoring their graduates was represented by their dean and the leading chair professor. Once all were seated on stage, the band began the playing a classic marching song. Stepping out from all the surrounding buildings, hundreds of professors in stately fashion entered the quadrangle and found their designated seat according to rank. Each professor proudly wore his or her long velvet robe with neck collars that displayed whatever eminent school from which they graduated and the degree obtained. Atop the head of each was the traditional mortarboard with multiple tassels signifying any honors achieved. The collage of color from all the professors as they entered the grassy field was an amazing sight to see. Excitement filled the air this late spring day. Everyone was now present. Each guest and family member was anxious for the graduates to enter and march down the long center aisle.

I was already sweating under the flowing, black robe adorned with neck banner signifying the school's colors. Green velvet was placed all the way down the front of the banner, attesting to my degree of a medical doctor. Like the professors, I was wearing a mortarboard with two tassels hanging from the right side, which frequently struck the side of my face as I walked. One of the tassels represented the university. The other was given by the medical school and had the two gold letters MD dangling from the side. Suddenly, the band stopped playing, and after a brief silence, kettle drums began a beat of a crescendo rolling cadence. To each side of the quadrangle were placed these large, bellowing percussion instruments. Alongside the percussionists was a brass section with French horns. Once the drum roll commenced, the horns announced with a bold declaration that the entrance of the graduates was to begin.

The medical doctors were the first to leave the student union building. I was told that the law school graduates were second in line. There was a rumor circulating around the university that several years back there had been a heated debate between the heads of the two professional schools. The disagreement centered on the decision as to which graduating class should walk out first in the commencement program. Would it not have been exciting to observe this epic battle? It seems doctors and lawyers are age-old adversaries. The debate ended in a draw, and the decision was made by the president of the university. The two would alternate years when designating which class came in first. Doctors were first on odd years, and lawyers were first on even years. I was pleased that on this day that we doctors had first footing. Behind the doctors and then the lawyers were the candidates receiving advanced degrees of masters and doctorates either in philosophy or science. The business and nursing schools were present, as well as the various departments such as biology, chemistry, philosophy, music, art, languages, and political science.

The actual awarding of degrees was performed in reverse order. So, the medical students were last to walk across the stage. To my delight, near the beginning of the procession were three of my old friends among the graduates being awarded the PhD in anatomy. I noticed that several of us pointed to these three as they walked past us. Our anatomy friends seemed pleased that we acknowledged them. They smiled at us in return, a sign of their mutual respect as they made their way to the stage.

My heart was full of pride knowing that I had completed something truly great. It was a day full of gratitude that had finally arrived. It was also a day of anticipation: my internship lay ahead, several weeks away. Many pictures were taken—several of my parents holding my diploma with huge smiles on their faces. I knew their partial financial support during the four years had been a burden, and I was so deeply grateful. On top of that, their emotional support was immeasurable. In fact, they were responsible for much of my success in my life. My mom and dad were always there when I needed them. Words of encouragement are never so dear as when they come from the loving heart of a parent. The small tears of joy upon a mother's cheek were priceless. The firm handshake from a proud father was a moment that will always nourish the soul.

My brow was sweating and my heart soaring. This day was so full of gratitude, not only for the many people who helped me get to this point, but in remembrance of the many others who were on another list. That list of nearly two thousand candidates who did not make it here. We were the lucky ones, the seventy-six of us seated, capped and gowned, and soon to be declared Doctor of Medicine. This was a good time to be humble, as well.

I thought of myself as that magnificent osprey my hermit friend described. This bird is like a king of the sky, riding currents of warm air almost effortlessly and eventually coming to rest upon his nest high above all the many creatures below. This day felt like a coronation after countless hours of training, days of faithfully waiting, and years of preparation.

Like most graduation ceremonies, there was much pageantry that preceded that actual awarding of degrees. All seventy-six of us were ordered to stand, proceed to the right side of the stage, and await our name to be called. Many of our teaching physicians formed a receiving line to right of the stage as we waited to walk up the steps onto the stage. There was Dr. Goldman, the cardiologist who told me that my heart will be just fine. Also, there in the receiving line, was Dr. Adolf Bourne, who terrorized us as freshman students in anatomy. Even though he did cast a smile to many of us, he still appeared threatening. And there was Dr. Johnston, the dean of admissions, who took the advice of his secretary and allowed me to speak to him late one summer day, four years ago.

The highlight of the commencement was when the president of the university called us out by name, and we walked across the stage. Each of us was handed the diploma by none other than Dean Dr. Johnston. How fitting this was for me. He was the first doctor to welcome me to the school and one of last to bid me farewell. In the next step, I shook the welcoming hand of the dean of the medical school. I looked directly into his dark eyes accentuated by his bushy, dark eyebrows as he told me, "Congratulations, Doctor Carpenter. It was a pleasure to have you here as a student."

I wanted so badly to finally ask him if he really had been a movie star in Hollywood, but his right brow moved slightly upward, as he was looking back at me as if to say, "Don't even try and ask me that question."

Instead I said respectfully, "Thank you, sir," before I walked off the stage.

At that moment, I saw my father standing fully erect with shoulders back and a firm set jaw. He was clapping vigorously, as if he wanted to proclaim to the world, "Yes, that's my son!" Next to him was my mom, her hands clasped in front of her face. Again, tears were streaming down her cheeks. In this moment she said not a word—probably couldn't have if she wanted to. She allowed her tears to say everything her heart was feeling.

This was one of those defining moments in life that would remain indelibly sketched in the mind forever. I took hold of the rail, looked to find the step, but stopped momentarily. Oh, what a feeling when time seems to stop, and you are standing atop the world. The flash bulbs were popping. My two nephews were jumping up and down and just barely able to hold themselves back from screaming and cheering out loud. I remember the tassels flying from the mortarboard and the sweat dripping off my face and down my back. What a memorable moment this became.

In another instant, I was flashing back to a similar day when I was sweating profusely in a phone booth and had just received the gift that was another defining moment in my life. A part of me wanted to jump off the stage into the exciting world that awaited me as a physician. I smiled, took a deep breath, and proceeded to slowly take the few remaining steps off the stage.

My reflection was broken instantly: my nephew could not withhold himself any longer, came running toward me, and jumped into my arms exclaiming, "You made it!"

The procession ended, and we could once more sit. After several words from various dignitaries, the commencement speaker was introduced. He was a prominent U. S. state senator. Like many commencement speakers, most of his speech was forgotten quickly. Most assuredly his thoughts and advice were profound; however, we the graduating class were anxious after four demanding years of training for the president of the university to return to the podium to decree the diploma granted. In all honesty, we could not think about anything else. I remembered only a few words from the thirty-minute commencement address, "Much of what is stated here today will be forgotten, but…" He told us to be bold, and he told us to be gentle. I liked this combination of valor. He concluded with wise words, "Have honor in everything you do and be of service to our fellow man." In that moment, he reminded me of my friend on his island back home.

I would soon wear the long white coat, which would signify to all that I had the MD behind my name. With this long coat, you walk a little slower. For the first time in your life you get a small monthly paycheck when you become an intern. Unlike a medical student, now your pockets have much less stuff in them. This, in some way, tells the world that memory cards are no longer needed; all the knowledge is in your head, ready to be utilized and shared with the third-year and fourth-year students.

So much for appearances; the truth was easily covered up by the long, white coat. There was so much more to learn. Knowledge was one thing when it's in the head as the student. Having that knowledge and putting it to use was another thing altogether. Conjuring this vast accumulation of understanding from the mind and applying it in real life was a daunting feat that every intern must learn over his year of training. Providing excellent care to the patient was the ultimate goal. Rendering care with compassion was an equally important task. The senator was correct when he said that boldness and gentleness will define one's career.

My graduation was unique because I not only had loving parents who acknowledged my accomplishment, but I also had a dear friend who was awaiting me back in his isolated home on the beach. His inspiring words had been replayed over and over in my head during many of the difficult times in my training. I looked forward to my return to his tranquil habitat on the island. This would be a perfect time to thank him for the many gifts that he had given me over these past few years. I could not wait to see my friend, the hermit, again.

CHAPTER 17

A Broken Shell

There were three weeks between graduation and the beginning of my internship. I chose to stay at the same teaching hospital where I had spent the past four years, and because the home of Mabel Levine had been so comfortable, I decided to stay with her for my internship year, as well. Before that, I would return home for a short visit and spend time with my parents and high school friends.

This visit revealed a unique passage in the life of a young doctor. For the first time when mail arrived, it was addressed to Dr. Carpenter. A secretary from my intern hospital called and said, "Good morning, Dr. Carpenter." Then my dad took me to see several of his American Legion buddies at the local breakfast cafe. I recall him saying, "Good morning, guys. Say hello to my son. I have told you about him? He is home for a short break before he starts his internship. This is Dr. Carpenter!" To hear yourself addressed as doctor for the first time aroused many mixed emotions. As one can imagine, it would take some time to adjust. I felt proud, obviously. But I was also humbled. It seemed a little embarrassing, even scary, knowing the burden of responsibility that came with the title. My Dad kept the conversation jovial. It was a great moment for a proud father. Fortunately, no one asked for medical advice.

The days quickly passed. The time with parents and old friends had been fun. The short summer vacation was about to end. What better time would there be and go to see my friend, the hermit?

I entered from the "front door", which traversed one of the thickest parts of the forest and led into the tunnel, which hid the closest entrance to the dwelling of the hermit. Finding the opening to the tunnel was a bit of a challenge since it had been covered with brush. There were a few remaining stones from the watch tower nearby, the key to finding the tunnel. He had told me on my last visit that only his "honored" friends could enter his home from this direction. Therefore, this made me a treasured friend! I hoped that this was the case.

Upon entering his encampment, I noticed that his things were in disarray. This was very unusual. The sand had not been raked, and palm limbs broken from their trunks were scattered about the opening.

As I walked into the sandy quadrangle, the hermit was sitting upon one of his stumps with his head hanging down. He appeared dejected and physically feeble for the first time. He looked up, nodded to me, smiled, and said that the winter had taken its toll on him. "It was harsh, but I survived," he said. "And I'll be happy to experience another summer. I'm a bit more tired now, but my spirits are improving with each day. I am so happy that you have come to visit me again! It has been sixteen and a half years on the island living with all these animal friends, but it is always special when a dear friend returns to share a story."

He invited me to sit upon the other stump. "It seems now that this is the December of one's life." With that familiar chuckle that I had heard so many times before he continued. "You know what comes at the end of the month of December? Why, it is Christmas! And Christmas is a very joyous occasion! Christmas is a time you should anticipate with great expectation!"

At the time, I was not completely sure of the exact meaning behind his analogy, but considering his present state, I was not convinced that his anticipated Christmas was something that I wanted to see come to be. It seemed strange, also, to speaking of Christmas in the height of summer!

We spent several hours together, mostly talking about my last year at school, graduation, and the anticipation of my internship. He advised me that I should "keep my feet on the ground" next year. He had a bad cough, but it never seemed to slow him down when something joyful came from his sunburned lips. He offered me a drink of berry juice that he had bottled in early spring. There was a subtle suggestion that the sugar content of the brew was beginning to ferment. The taste was still good, so together we drank. I gave him his gifts of apples, zucchini seeds, and a loaf of home-made bread from my mom's kitchen. This time he had made no request for a book.

He was thankful as always and then settled down again upon his favorite stump and began to dispense these precious words of advice, "My dear friend, do not ever forget what has been spoken here at this place. Make these words of wisdom a part of your spirit and these thoughts will prolong your life and fill it with meaning. Wisdom and an honorable life lived in service to others will give you happiness. Let your caring for all living things never falter. Let your love be like a chain around your neck that you never remove. Write these words in your heart, you will have joy and peace. Be content with what the world has provided. Look only at what you have and not with what you have not. Only then will you be aware that you live abundantly."

Standing and surveying his comfortable encampment, he continued, "Find truth in nature. Observe all of creation and be aware of its Creator. Do not lean too heavily on your own thoughts. Do not elevate yourself too high in your own eyes." The teacher took a deep breath and a swallow of berry juice. "By being in union with all living things, you will find strength and comfort. Honor your fellow man and share your wealth with them. With the labor of your work be joyful. In so doing, your home will be filled with blessings, and you will never want for anything in life. These truths will open a gate, and you be able to follow a path of fulfilment."

I was captivated by his words of profound wisdom. The hermit walked to the heavy metal door of his dwelling, entered it, and then returned handing me some dried beans to chew. "Suffering will occur. Think of it as your discipline. Do not judge suffering as bad. To all men, trial and tribulation is given as a gift, much like the father delightfully gives knowledge to his child. You will find joy in knowing that this gift of suffering will give you true understanding. It will make you wise among others. This knowledge will return you more than silver and gold. It will be more precious than fine jewels." He hesitated briefly, as if he knew that I needed a moment to gather my thoughts. "Nothing can compare to the wisdom you will possess, when you discover that you can have a personal relationship with your creator. Living with these trials becomes tolerable. You will realize that they cause you to grow. Your spirit will be filled with passion. Your life will seem complete, and you will embrace calmness." The hermit smiled as he walked over to an oak at the edge of the clearing. He bent over and firmly held its trunk. "Nature's wisdom is the tree of life for those of us who chose to live within it. You will be blessed if you adhere to its teachings. Listen to this my dear friend: you must be in the world, and you must participate in it." The hermit took another sip and after a moment of silence, spoke with a stern determination, "But you do not have to be of this world!"

He then stood up straight and looked up into the sky. He started to swirl his arms in the air and appeared light of foot, as if he were about to break into song. "It is from perfect wisdom that a creator first set the earth in its orbit. It is a gift to see the world's diversity. The oceans were first divided up, and the land was to be replenished by the rain from the clouds. Oh, what a beautifully designed blueprint it is!"

The hermit sat down once more upon his stump. "Protect your freedom to choose your path. Keep this wisdom close to you, and you will live abundantly. You will be able to go out in this world and feel safe, and you will not stumble. When you rest you will not be afraid, and you will sleep well."

His voice softened, "Be kind to all living things when you are able to do so. If their loss must be, then let it be for the necessity of survival. Do not pass judgment nor falsely accuse any person when they have done you harm. Do not take joy in any unkind action! Always choose kindness, and others will follow. Know that an unkind person is loathsome. Only the kind will gain. The self-righteous will be mocked. Be forever humble and you will walk next to your fellow man with joy and peace in your heart."

I had to ask him a question. I had to slow him down a bit so that I could take this all in, "From everything you have told me, what should I remember when I become a physician?"

It appeared that I had not broken his train of thought because he replied in the same cadence as before, "There are two rules that govern those who choose to live and be among other people. First, you must respect everyone and their actions. This includes respecting yourself and doing your part. And second, you must respect and care for all living things as if they were the same as yourself. You are to have dominion over them, but you do not own them. By living with this honor, you will live with joy."

The hermit was growing weary. "We have spoken at great lengths for many years. By learning these ways of life and how the many animals and plants live together in harmony and balance, one can also learn to live with one's fellow man. It is easy to lose oneself in the cyclic patterns of life. It is especially true when living alone on this island. With much patience and awareness, you become a part of the world in which you live."

I reached into the bag of dried beans and scooped out another hand full for a tasty chew. I had eaten quite a few and noted that the bag was almost empty. As I continued to chew on the beans, I wanted to apologize for eating all of his bounty, but the hermit interrupted me and began to speak again, "If you have been paying attention during every one of your visits here, you would have noticed that the words spoken in conversation here are never in the first person. Before today, you have never heard the use of 'I' nor 'me' from these lips. With practice, the 'I and 'me' do not exist in one's vocabulary. Why do this? It is done initially to help one become void of the self. Getting rid of the self is essential to survival when living separate from the human world and alone with only the many plants and animals on this island. You cannot live separate from the rest of the island's living creatures. You cannot constantly dwell in your own needs or wants. A small beach sparrow sits on the back of a deer and awaits a horse fly that wants to bite the deer. The bird eats the fly for lunch, and the deer is not plagued by the irritating fly. The two live in peaceful, symbiotic harmony. There is no 'I', and there is no 'me' when living on this island. All live interdependently."

With these words, the hermit stood and looked straight into my eyes and for the first time in all these years, he spoke in the first person,

"My friend, *I* give you this as a gift as a reminder of the wisdom you have gained from this island. You have been listening to *me* for a long time." He then took off the necklace with the single broken shell that had always hung around his neck. "This is a simple broken shell that once lay upon the shoreline being tumbled by the endless waves, much like the countless other broken shells alongside it. This shell was once a part of a thriving animal that lived its days next to its neighbors until its inevitable death. In the December of its life, it was cast upon the shoreline. With the force of the many breaking waves, this shell grew smaller and smaller. Eventually, it would have been reduced to scattered grains of sand. It once appeared as just one of millions along the shore. Later in time, a person would have seen just another unwanted and unappreciated speck of sand to be washed from their daughter's back. However, this clam shell is unique among so many. This shell is different—unlike any other in form, size, and color. Likewise, you are one of a kind among many. You must take this chain. May you wear this broken shell in remembrance that it is one of millions on the shoreline, but in its own time and form is special and unique just like you."

With these thoughts, he walked to his pill box home, opened the door, turned to me, and by gesturing with his hand invited me inside. For the first time since I had known him, I was granted a view of the interior of his home. What I was about to see was as unique as the shell around my neck.

Upon entering through the large metal door, there was a central room with a long table. I imagined this was originally intended for the army troops to have their meals upon. Candles were carefully placed along the table to evenly light the room. The hermit had adorned the table neatly with objects from his surroundings. They were arranged as if each grouping was some type of experiment or project he was working on. To the back of the room was a much smaller table with two wooden chairs. A cabinet lined one wall and was full of all types of food products. At the back of the central room was a cistern from which water could be drawn. To the left in a small room were two sets of bunk beds. The lower bed was made up neatly with pillows and blanket. Off the right of the main room was a den with a cozy chair, small wooden desk, and two large bookcases neatly stacked with books. As I looked more closely at row after row of books, many had note cards or pieces of paper placed between pages. The titles suggested books on various topics ranging from eastern religions to agriculture, classical novels to biographies of past presidents.

"Do you have the same problem—that there's never enough time to read everything you want?" He asked as he walked toward the back wall, reached for the handle of the cistern, and retrieved some water. He held two glasses firmly. "We are both hungry for knowledge. For many years now we both have read many books about worldly things and have arrived at a point that we believe that we understand the workings of the world."

He passed me a glass of pure, cold water. "It is not until you drink from the eternal, the supernatural waters that you have rebirth, and obtain divine knowledge. It is then that you become aware of the timeless and selfless wonder of the divine plan. There is a connectedness to all of life. The creator of this world does not speak with words taught through human wisdom contained in these many books. However, you are given spiritual truths as a gift if you have faith and allow yourself to believe. Should you come to the point that you trust this Divine understanding and do not rely on your own insight, you can learn the true ways of life." With the pure water from his cistern, we toasted each other and drank.

After an hour of quietly roaming through his many books together, we made our way to the front door. As he was showing me out he said, "I want you listen closely to this. You know my young friend, you have but three paths to choose from. First, you can choose evil and mean ways of doing things. There are bad spirited people in the world. This will not likely ever be a choice for you. The second path leads you to doing good works and good deeds. This path will keep you busy. At some point, after many years of labor, you will ask yourself, 'What is all this worth?' Many people choose this path in life. But there is a third, much less traveled path that gives outstanding truth. It is these gifted few who choose to drink from the well of pure spiritual waters, quench their thirst for knowledge, and live a life full of anticipation, passion, and purpose. They live connected yet separate from the rest of the creation around them."

We stood in the light of a setting sun, and he said farewell. "Believing in what your spiritual heart speaks to you and having faith in something much larger than yourself will make your life seem as if you are floating down a river. There will be turbulence along the way. Even *I* have experienced a few rapids. But the waters of faith will buoy you and keep you afloat. Choosing the river, the path of spiritual awareness, you will live a life of · unbelievable achievement. You will enjoy true joy in this world, despite the occasional suffering. You will find and see this Godly kingdom that is among you while on this earth." The hermit pointed me toward the setting sun and with tears swelling up in his eyes told me, "You have been a dear friend, and we will both miss the other until we meet again. Now, go and choose your own path."

My mind was racing. I wanted to remember every word. I could only imagine how tranquil his life must have been each evening as he settled down to escape into another mystery that all his books would unravel. As I focused in on his wrinkled face that weather and time had so well sculpted, I remembered his subtle remarks regarding the December of his life and that Christmas was about to arrive. He had also referred to the shells on the beach, their eventual decay. He had spoken about the marsh grasses and how it eventually turns into the piles of detritus along the shore. All of this suggested a pattern of life to death and back to life; perhaps he was referring to the cycle of life. Then, I remembered how poorly he himself had weathered the previous winter and the disarray I had noticed upon arriving. I was coming to the concerning realization that the hermit may be saying his goodbyes forever.

Then, before I left the clearing and out of my own self-interest,

I turned to the hermit. "Thank you for everything. But, have you forgotten that you promised me that you would share the 'way' to selflessness? You said there was a gate that you would describe. You said that the gate led to a narrow path. You said that I must be given this information only when I became a doctor." I paused for a moment and said, "I am a doctor now!"

"*I* will tell you what you must know. I will share with you what you desire. I have not brought you to this point only to abandon you. I am your friend. I will feed you what you need. I am aware that you have obtained your degree. I know that you are a doctor; however, I am also aware that you are not yet a clinician. I tell you now that you need another year to become a doctor who can care for his patient. I am aware that timing is important when imparting certain knowledge. For this reason and given that it is again late in the day, I will not share any more with you today." He laughed and his whole countenance changed in a second. "I am also aware that your mom has a home cooked meal waiting for you when you return tonight. Please extend my thanks to her for the homemade bread." As he was about to close the door to his quarters, a sad expression came upon his face. "Farewell, I look forward to seeing you upon your return."

I had never heard the hermit use the word "I" so much. In a way it seemed out of character, but in another sense, it felt warm and familiar. I felt closer to him than ever before. Our relationship had grown. Without a doubt, I must return after my internship year.

I chose the path leaving his home facing the setting sun as he had encouraged. There was a finality in his words that haunted me. These words along with the setting sun casted long shadows both in my mind and on my body. I took my time getting home. In my heart something was telling me that the shadows from the hermit were also growing longer. As I approached home I thought, "Could it be that the hermit has forgotten his final words of wisdom about the gate? Perhaps he wants me to find it out for myself? The next year will reveal all. I will learn how to care for a patient and become a clinician. Without question when this year is over, I will return to the hermit."

CHAPTER 18

Wearing the Long White Coat

There was no real vacation between graduation and the beginning of the internship year. Mrs. Levine was happy to see me and pleased to know that she would have me around for another year. In no time, I was back in the hospital and rounding on the patients on "my" service. I had been given a taste of having my own patients when I worked as an acting intern in my fourth year of medical school and had enjoyed the responsibility. I also had developed a special interest in surgery after taking an elective in orthopedics that same year; therefore, I elected to take a rotating surgical internship. I was given the duties of an intern on the services of urology, gynecology, and otolaryngology. I was given two elective rotations, and I chose thoracic surgery and orthopedics.

In each specialty, as an intern, you were responsible for the "work-up" of each patient scheduled for surgery. This included doing a history and physical, ordering the appropriate lab studies, and x-rays required prior to the surgical procedure. Each day began at 5 AM, making chart rounds and collecting lab and x-ray results. After gathering the information, you would enter each patient's room, introduce yourself again to the patient and family members, make sure the patient was prepared for surgery, and address any last-minute concerns. The surgical consent form had to be signed, and we had to make sure that nothing was taken by mouth so that the anesthesiologist could administer general anesthesia.

At 6 AM, you would join up with your team, which consisted of the attending surgeon, chief resident of service, a first-year or second-year resident, the intern, and one or two third-year or fourth-year medical students. Once the team was assembled, the second-year resident would be responsible for directing the rounding on patients. The team would enter each patient's room, and the intern would report the status of the patient, recite the significant results of lab studies and x-rays, and relay any concerns of the patient or the family members. At this point, the chief resident would ask a few questions and determine if the patient was a "go" and therefore ready for surgery. Then, as the entire team filed out of the room, either the chief resident or the attending surgeon would begin the discussion by directing questions to members of the team pertaining to the diagnosis or prognosis.

"Does this patient have any allergies to medications?"

Immediately the intern would respond with confidence, "The patient is allergic to penicillin."

The next question would be fired at the intern by the attending surgeon, "Doctor, do you think we should use Ancef, a cephalosporin, as your post-operative antibiotic?"

The well-prepared intern, who had read about the use of cephalosporin as the choice of antibiotics after sinus surgery could choose his words wisely, "There is reported only a 7-10% cross allergic response with Ancef and penicillin allergic patients. Most physicians elect to use this medication as a safe and effective post-surgical antibiotic choice." The attending would then ask the second-year resident, "Well, what if the patient had a documented anaphylactic response to penicillin and started having trouble breathing?"

The scholarly resident would jump in and respond, "Anaphylaxis is considered a relative contraindication for the use of cephalosporins in penicillin allergic patients."

Each member of the team would be confronted and expected to respond. In so doing, hopefully, he would display the depth of his knowledge relative to the point in question. You can imagine that the tension was extremely high for everyone, except for the attending and chief resident. It was only during the surgical procedure that the attending would fire questions at the chief resident and expect perfection.

If, however, any member of the team answered a question hesitantly or responded slowly, suggesting uncertainty, then they were setting themself up for embarrassing, pointed questions. You learned quickly that it was better to say, "I do not know." The attending would look at you with that stare of rejection, but things would return to normal shortly. The learning curve was high.

This is the life of every young intern. Yes, he is a doctor, but he is not yet a clinician.

Most of the time, everyone on the team worked with precision. I do recall on one occasion, the fourth-year student forgot to type and cross two units of blood for a patient who was to have a bowel resection. It was my responsibility to double check, and it was the second-year resident's responsibility to check after me. The chief resident was responsible overall. This happened only once. The patient did well during the surgery and fortunately for him and us no blood was required that day. This kind of error was unacceptable and therefore never occurred again. Everyone received the firm reprimand and moved on. Some skills are learned through failures. This can be unfortunate for the patient; however, this is the time-honored method in which young doctors fine tune the complex skills of becoming a clinician.

Considerable repetition is also required to learn the skills needed to care for patients. Imagine an early morning on each hall of a teaching hospital. Six, maybe seven teams, stand just outside a patient's room in the hallways of each floor of the hospital. Multiple dialogues of clinical and academic discussions are being conducted simultaneously. All these people stirring about and the volume of voices speaking simultaneously causes the hallways to come alive with a buzz. It could seem somewhat chaotic, but this dramatic scene is well orchestrated. For years, this drama has played out daily in the lives of young physicians. This manner of learning has proven to produce excellent, caring physicians for generations of patients.

Once the surgery was over, afternoon rounds with the chief resident would occur. When the afternoon rounds concluded, the intern and medical students would divide up and complete the duties. Around 6-8 PM, you would find your way to the library or find a quiet corner in the hospital to study. This was the time to prepare for whatever different and challenging surgical cases were scheduled the next morning. You would have to read about the surgical procedure itself and be prepared for any possible adverse outcomes. Each member of the team must be prepared with the answers related to care for that day's patients—day after day. The year seems to speed by, and before you know it, you are preparing for your next year of responsibilities.

The internship is all about time management. For the first time in your career, you are expected to make treatment decisions regarding your patient. Of course, there are the residents and attending faculty available, if you can manage to catch their attention. If you ask the right question, at the right time, then you are likely to receive helpful answers to your dilemma. Otherwise, you are on your own with stacks of textbooks as your late-night companions. There are the times when you present your patient on rounds in the morning and totally screw up. You are quickly advised of the correct plan of treatment. It can be embarrassing and sometimes downright humiliating. Despite the many ups and downs, this sink or swim manner of training the medical intern has stood the test of time. You learn to manage this six day a week, fourteen hours a day schedule at the hospital. You gain confidence, learn sound patient care, and develop an appropriate level of humility.

There are so many patients. There is so much to do each day. There is so much to learn. Quickly, you discover that there is so much you do not know! Fortunately, your energy seems limitless. Unfortunately, your time is the scarce commodity. The year does march on, and with each day comes unique learning experiences. When the year is complete, you realize that you have learned a tremendous amount about patient care. You are excited ready to move onward and upward.

The wearing of the long white coat was the symbol that you are a doctor with MD behind your name. The wearing of the coat was hard earned, but it had its honor. At the end of a year as an intern, stains from every imaginable viscous agent and every viable liquid expressed by the human body had tarnished this once pure, white coat. These stains, like the metals worn on the chest of military officers, were worn as badges of honor for the intern called to duty.

For me, another medallion was worn around my neck, a unique aged shell given to me by someone special. This necklace was worn with honor, as well. It reminded me of the hermit's sound wisdom, which had helped me to live through difficult times.

CHAPTER 19

A Time to Surrender

There was a short two-week break between the internship year and the first year of residency. The year had flown by, and it seemed like just days since I was here on the shoreline anxiously waiting to see my dear friend, the hermit. I still wore the shell around my neck. It had come to represent a sense of calm, awareness, and belonging to me. It reminded me of the hermit himself.

For the first time, I feared what he would look like on this visit. He had aged so much in the past two years. I hoped that his winter was mild and he had weathered the season better this time around. I attempted to enter by way of the front entrance that turned from the shore. To my surprise, the tunnel was barricaded with sand.

"How strange," I thought. The hermit was fastidious in keeping his dwelling well-kept.

With some concern, I took the back route. I crossed the spit, traversed the mud flats, and approached the hermit's home by way of the bay side entrance. Throughout my journey, I was fearful of what I may find at the hermit's home. It took a long time to arrive because the tide was high and the mud was deep.

I finally reached the open quadrangle in front of his pill box home. My concern increased as I saw tree limbs strewn across the clearing. The area seemed even more unkempt than last time. The stump upon which I usually found the hermit was empty. I searched outside, but he was nowhere to be found. I called out for him, but the only response was that of a seagull flying high above. I decided to check inside his bunker. Again, he was nowhere to be found, although the bunker seemed to be in order. I sat in his wooden desk chair and waited for his return for nearly an hour. The silence and serenity created by the flickering of the candles I had lit and placed on the table spoke to me and said that he was not coming home.

He was gone from this place. I imagined that his life's candle had been blown out by the winter's blistering cold winds. I sensed that his spirit was also gone from this room. I stared at the many books that lined the walls of his den. I imagined that he had many close friends like myself who brought these books for him to read. I realized that he must have taken his other friends on a journey of self-discovery like the one he and I had taken together.

My mind wandered for some time. Then, I noticed several stacks of books on the table in the center of the main room. I stood up to investigate and found dozens of Bibles. Inside each of the Bibles was a piece of paper inserted between specific pages to point out a special passage. At the top of each bookmark, peeking out of the Bible, was a name. I began to search, hoping that I would find a Bible with my name on one of the pieces of paper. I was beginning to give up when finally, in the next to last stack, the third Bible down, I noticed my name. As I removed this Bible from the stack, I was amazed that it was the very same Bible that he had requested I bring to him. Inside the front cover were the words that I had written to him:

To my friend, thank you for our time together.

With trembling fingers, I opened to the first bookmark. A piece of paper fell into my hand. Scribbled in the hermit's writing were these words:

The December of my life is here, and when I awake in the morning, Christmas will be here. This celebration will be like no other that I have experienced on this island. Although I wish to sleep now, I also dearly yearn for the morning of Christmas to occur. I wait like a child! I will see you again on your appointed life's December and your life's Christmas morning. Farewell my friend.

My Bible was bookmarked to Matthew. A passage was circled, Matthew 16:24-26. With tears in my eyes and a trembling voice, I read the passage aloud:

> 24 The Jesus said to his disciples, "Whoever wants to be my disciple must deny themselves and take up their cross and follow me. 25 For whoever wants to save their life will lose it, but whoever loses their life for me will find it. 26 What good will it be for someone to gain the whole world, yet forfeit their soul."

My dear friend had given me one last gift. I reread the passage and thought about its meaning. What did he want me to learn from this passage? I noticed that there was another bookmark. It was labeled "#2." I turned the pages and opened to John 21, verses 15-19. They read:

> 15 When they had finished breakfast, Jesus said to Simon Peter, "Simon son of John, do you love me more than these?" He said to him, "Yes, Lord; you know that I love

you." Jesus said to him, "Feed my lambs." 16 A second time he said to him, "Simon son of John, do you love me?" He said to him, "Yes, Lord; you know that I love you." Jesus said to him, "Tend my sheep." 17 He said to him the third time, "Simon son of John, do you love me?" Peter felt hurt because he said to him the third time, "Do you love me?" And he said to him, "Lord, you know everything; you know that I love you." Jesus said to him, "Feed my sheep. 18 Very truly, I tell you, when you were younger, you used to fasten your own belt and to go wherever you wished. But when you grow old, you will stretch out your hands, and someone else will fasten a belt around you and take you where you do not wish to go." 19 After this he said to him, "Follow me."

Again, I puzzled over what this dear friend was trying to teach me. The first passage spoke of life and death. Perhaps, he was referring to his own. The second passage puzzled me. Why did Jesus keep asking Peter if he loved Him? Each time he answered, Jesus responded, "Feed my sheep." What did that mean?

I was convinced that the hermit had given me another gift. However, his motive was confusing. Was he trying to tell me "to live you must die"? What does "Feed my sheep" have to do with me? I had more questions than answers. I wanted to understand this final message from my old friend. Somehow it gave me hope that I would be able to keep the hermit alive in my heart. I thought to myself, "follow me" at the end of the message must be significant.

In the very next moment, I noticed a notation that had been written on the second bookmark which read:

Charles, I have one remaining and important gift for you. Please look under my bed and you will find the stool *that we spoke about. You may have this stool as your own. There is also something else for you under the stool that you must read.*

I picked up a candle and walked briskly to his bunk bed. Sure enough, sitting upside down was the stool just as he had said. Under the stool was a sealed envelope with my name on the front. I sat down on the bunk, placed the candle on his bedside stand, and opened the envelope. The letter read:

My dear Charles, I am aware that you have been asking for the truth that will lead you to the fulfillment of that blessed state of selflessness. I know that I have taken you on a long journey. Do you remember the first time that we spoke about the three-legged stool? You remember that the stool is symbolic of stability. For you to have stability, purpose, and meaning in life, you must strive for three things. The first two legs seem obtainable, even in this world of distractions. We are physical beings, and we are made to have duties and work. Work is essential to a sense of purpose. Equally important, we are emotional beings, and we are made to feel things. Love, being the greatest of all emotions, is essential. Without it in your daily endeavors, a life would have no meaning.

Then, the final leg represented the soul. In order to have meaning, we must deal with our own immorality, determine a way to deal with our sinful nature, and find a way to have a relationship with our creator. We concluded from our discussions that the only way to reconcile this seemingly impossible task of securing our necessary third leg is to have a heart full of humility. We said we must seek selflessness. I left you with the idea that getting to this point is like finding and walking through a narrow gate with a path on the other side. Remember, I told you that you would be more prepared to accept the final truth once you finished your internship year?

It saddens me greatly not to be here with you to share this wisdom. As we have said previously, timing is important.

The time is now right to continue our discussion and search for the understanding of this third leg: selflessness.

I thought to myself, "Finally, I am going to have the key to unraveling this quest for selflessness. He is right. It has been two years since I first encountered the notion of the three-legged stool." The hermit's writing continued:

There is a gate sought by many. Few ever do discover it. What is it like? What does it look like? Well, you must enter alone. All your possessions must be left behind. Once you find the path, it is easy to step to the right or the left and fall off the narrow path. But the path is the only one that leads to selflessness. It is the way of humility.

You have asked me several times to tell you just what you must do to have this understanding, find the true purpose in life, and find your way to meaning and stability in life. I have hesitated to share this final truth with you. It was not that I did not want to share it, but honestly, it was not until a few weeks ago that I myself fully arrived at complete understanding of this teaching. I confess to you that I came to this island many years ago to live in solitude with my plant and animal friends and to find my own three-legged stool. The work became routine and quite enjoyable. The love for the friends who surrounded me was easy to secure. The third leg, that elusive leg, has taken a lifetime here to fully comprehend. I have realized that my coming here was more selfish than selfless. I came to protect myself from the hurts of the world, but in turn I removed myself from people whom I could reach and narrowed my world to the people who reached me.

I wanted to jump to the next page of his writing. Did he have to struggle with death to come to this understanding? What must I do to finally understand all that he is saying? How do I find my way on this path and not fall off? I turned to the next page:

My dear Charles, this is what I want you to know. There is absolutely NOTHING that you can DO to achieve this way!

What you seek is impossible with man. What you desire is possible only with God. You ask why this is so? I have spoken of an evil force in the world. One can best and simply describe this harmful reality as man's sinful nature. Man constantly commits acts against others to gain the upper hand, to have control. We are, after all, in competition with everyone and everything for the pleasures of this world, which appear to be both desirable and scarce. Man covets, lies, finds fault, steals, and even murders.

However, the most subtle, most dangerous, and most universal sin is against the self. It is called pride. Pride is the greatest enemy to selflessness or humility. God gave us all a great gift, and it is called free-will. With this ability to choose, we almost always desire the self and our own pleasures over others. Man has a great love affair with himself. With this freedom, we come to believe that we can accomplish anything, defeat anyone, if only we are willing to work hard enough to obtain it. We need no one. We believe that we are islands unto ourselves. I have learned from living on this island that nothing could be farther from the truth!

I realized that I was still no closer to the answer than I was before. If this was true, then there was nothing I could do.

Furthermore, if I worked harder or made any effort on my own to attain the stability of a three-legged stool, then my self-serving pride would get in the way. I got it!

It's impossible to achieve any meaning in life! Wait, was that right? What good is all this? It's just philosophical babble!

I looked down at the pages. There was one more handwritten page from the hermit to read. With anxious fingers I flipped the page and read:

OK, I can imagine that you are about to give up on this old man's advice, about to run away and never return. However, though the narrow path may twist and turn, it does continue. There is a way down the path even though it becomes darkened, limited, and seemingly impossible to traverse. Charles, you must surrender!

And Charles, herein lies the hard part. The surrender must be total and absolute. Any little piece of the self that you retain for yourself can—in your sinful, prideful nature—become a treasure that you covet and in turn lead you away from the true joy found in the hidden life of selflessness.

Whatever you choose to do with this question of surrender it is vitally important that it must come from the heart. You may know all about surrender in your head, but you must feel it in your heart. God is not so much concerned about what we do for Him.

He is more concerned about the condition of your heart. Charles, if you could be mature in your obedience to him...

You must walk your path alone, and no one, including me, should give you advice that may lead you astray. All that you will ever need beyond what I have suggested is in the book. Seek understanding, ask for help, knock at the gated door, and lean not on your own wisdom or efforts. May your path be clear and your way straight. You have taught me much. Farewell, my friend.

Remember—You must surrender!

I took my Bible, the stool, and his note with me. I dared not open the other Bibles there for they were for others to read who had been blessed by this gifted man. I glanced around his pill box home. Material things occupied much of his home, but his vibrant spirit was truly gone. This moment was hard to bear. I opened the large metal door, exited his now quiet home, and shut the door behind me. I never looked back.

On my way out, I remembered the other pill box, the hermit's closet. I decided to investigate for any clues to the hermit's last days. I reached the old military ammunition storage entrance, lit the candle that was next to the door, and noticed that all the hermit's possessions were just as I had seen them previously. I cautiously stepped across the circular room to the tunnel entrance and walked down the steps. I took several steps into the narrow tunnel and noticed that there was sand on the floor. I stopped and with my outreached arm, which was holding the candle, I stared in front of me.

There was a wall of sand completely obstructing the narrow

chamber. "Now, I realize why I could not enter through the hermit's front door. He must have spent his last days and hours in this hallway. He must have known his time was coming to an end. For his body to stay hidden forever in this place, he barricaded himself into the tunnel and took his last breath." The reality of this saddened me. "I will never see his wrinkled and kind face again."

I turned around and walked out of the storage closet. I closed the door, made my way to the clearing, and stopped. The wind had blown more debris into the sandy yard. No longer was it neatly raked and pristine to the eye. Nature was already starting to take back what was once cultivated by a very wise man. It was difficult to leave this place. Oh, if I could only see him one more time!

I thought of his gentle but rough-skinned face as I solemnly made my way to the shoreline. I sat down at the ocean's edge and kicked off my shoes and socks, letting the salty waves lap at my feet. I reflected on my past year of internship and realized how quickly time had elapsed. Now, as the gentle waves rhythmically bathed my feet, it appeared to me that time was moving very slowly. There was a calmness about me, as if nothing else mattered but the waves cooling my feet. I noticed the pelican bobbing up and down by the marching of waves a few yards out to sea. A ghost crab was repairing his buried home in the sand just to my left. To my right, there was a teenaged girl playing at the water's edge with her dad. They were hitting the volleyball back and forth to each other as if the day would never end. And a young couple, probably just married, walked hand in hand down the beach. They strolled slowly, intimately talking to one another, never aware of the others around them.

I started to dig a hole with my feet, something I had always done when in deep thought and sitting at the shoreline. I took hold of the shell around my neck as I looked down and noticed the millions of similar broken shells lying scattered in the sand. Each one was as unique as the one around my neck, each a memory of a past life. Each one was completing its own cycle of life, ultimately returning to the ocean's floor as another grain of sand. An hour elapsed. I stood up and started walking back down the beach toward my home.

Suddenly, my heart was full of joy. My mind was thinking of all the kindness I had witnessed during my visits with the hermit. The small shells beneath my body's weight made a familiar, soft crunch. Again, I imagined the sound coming from the breaking of tiny little bones under my feet. I held my precious shell firmly as if to protect it. Then, I stopped in my tracks. The sound of breaking shells stopped, as well. I was in the moment. I was aware of myself. I was aware of my surroundings. Despite the occasional cry of a solitary gull above, my stillness made a void of sounds. My senses became keenly aware of the background music, a beating rhythmic sound that I had also heard before. It was the sound of the waves washing upon the shore. Several minutes went by, and I started to reflect on all that I had read and seen today. I began to walk, slowly at first. I became keenly aware of all that I needed to understand.

I have my whole life ahead of me. I have an amazing career awaiting me. I have the last words from the hermit urging me to find the right way. I began to run full stride away from the shore, leaving behind the millions of broken shells that lay at my feet.

I was running home.
I was running toward my new life as a physician.
I was running down the path of the rest of my life.
I was running with the knowledge of years of training.
I was running with the wisdom from the hermit.
I was running with a heart full of burning passion.
I was running with kindness growing in my character.

I was running with the memory of one who lived
by example.
I was running with an emblem of a unique life
around my neck.
With one hand firmly gripping a Bible.
With the other holding on to a three-legged stool.
With questions that needed answers.
I was running my life's chosen path.

But I could not stop thinking about these three words that the
hermit had shared with me. They resounded and resonated in my
mind repeatedly. He had said:

"You must surrender!"

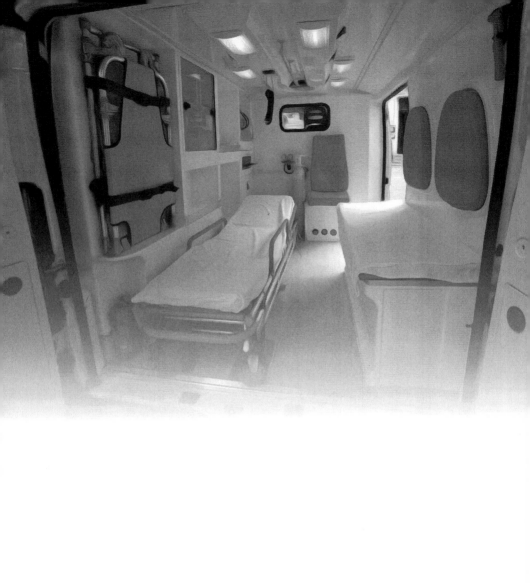

EPILOGUE

The fantasy life of the hermit must be addressed. There once was a real hermit who was the inspiration for this book. He lived in an abandoned military bunker on the shore of North Carolina from 1956 to June 1972. He lived alone and survived off what he was able to harvest from the land. Many people came to see him. These visits have been well documented by the individuals so fortunate to have witnessed the life of the hermit. The circumstances of his death are unclear. The bunker in which he lived for sixteen years still stands today. The quotation on his memorial reads:

> "You have what the world lacks,
> The courage to live by your own standards,
> And go your own way.
> This is the life that some dream
> But do not dare."

One can only imagine what his life was like. A "gift" was given to you through his imaginary voice. His thoughts were truths that everyone can hold close to heart.

At the beginning of this story, the reader was instructed to be aware of the exemplum, a story teaching a moral lesson or point. The moral point in this instance was about surrender and selflessness. The hermit suggested that it was impossible to become totally selfless by your own doing. He gave many gifts but also conceded it was not about the giver. Nor was it about the gifts.

He discovered that it was all about giving from the heart.

As the story of the hermit ended, the young physician was left running toward his future with hopes held high. However, inside his pounding heart, many questions persisted in equal measure. There were still truths to be discovered, beliefs to be instilled. What remains to be shared is the answer to the question, what happened to the young doctor in the rest of his life? Through the many twists and turns in his life, after all those patients seen, did the young doctor ever ascertain what the maxim *"you must surrender"* truly means?

With humility I must say that during his life, on occasion, he acted as if he was afraid of it. Perhaps, he was acting much like the rich, young ruler unwilling to give up his worldly treasures. To him it appeared to be too big a risk to surrender.

Forty-nine years of caring for the needs of patients have passed since the young man sat on those granite steps and waited. The passion of that day with its sultry weather and climatic moments remained so vivid in his mind. Looking back, that day was epic, not only effectively changing a young man's life but having consequences for thousands of patients who came into his care.

The ripple effect of that day has led him not to sitting on granite steps but resting on a pile of red Kenyan soil bricks. Each of these interlocking bricks was made by mixing an exact formula of soil, water, and cement, and then compressing it with a simple machine. The intensity of sun, after just three weeks, literally cooked these red bricks, making them ready for use in construction.

Being only twenty miles from the equator, the sun is brutal and burns the skin at midday, but things quickly cool down as it sinks into the horizon. The sunburnt grassy savannah of central Kenya is awe-inspiring. This wide-open frontier spans many miles and eventually reaches the mountain range with Mount Kenya towering over the valley below. Most days, clouds form over Mount Kenya around midday, hiding its majestic silhouette. Late in the afternoon, a small shower will pass through and settle the dust. This is the Africa that he always imagined, wild and untamed. This is a land patrolled only by an occasional lion and a three-thousand-pound hippo ruling over their respective environments.

This predictable sequence of weather patterns and the beauty of this unique area of the world is now familiar because his career is winding down to retirement, and a new life is unfolding. It was once shocking to say that he had become a missionary in Kenya. Now, he works part time in a rural community serving a small group of shepherds, farmers, and preachers. These faraway places and exciting adventures make his retirement enchanting.

He now sits upon the left-over bricks from the construction of the buildings of the mission project. Oh, how those "ripples in the water" that started from the day a scared and desperate student sat on those hot granite steps have produced a stunning cascade of events.

His life followed a wandering path. It started out fully immersed in a church. He went to college and was confronted with more liberal, worldly doctrines. Some of his strong beliefs were shaken. Then, he entered medical school where the beliefs of the scientific world led him far away from faith. The scientific world demanded that if a statement was to be true, then it must be proven. He read about world religions and even dove into self-help and self-discovery books, but he was still left with questions.

Somehow, he returned to reading the Bible. He was led to a man who told him to not just read it but *wrestle* with it. He studied and made notes, just as he had done in college and medical school. Soon, he began to find the truth in those pages. He took small steps in faith and it all started to fall into place. He came to the fundamental conclusion that the spiritual and the scientific worlds do not have to be contradictory but could be complimentary to each other. The two could live together like the black belly bird and the white belly bird that shared the skies on the seacoast. After a long wrestling match, he started to appreciate the importance of selflessness and complete surrender.

Was that last remaining position given to the most deserving candidate? Did seat number 76 out of 2,005 live up to expectations?

Can anyone respond to these questions? On occasion, I have attempted to answer them. Now, sitting on these red bricks, it seems unbelievable and too good to be real. There may never be a better time to resolve these issues. It took courage and big steps in faith to arrive at this place with this story to tell. Everyone loves to tell the stories of their life. I am no different than anyone else.

For most of those forty-nine years, I worked as an emergency physician. I saw people when they were experiencing one of the worst days in their lives. My view of human nature was most assuredly unique. If I became an expert at anything, it would have been the study of how individuals deal with stress, manage their fears, and attempt to find hope in their lives. There was so much pain. So much heartache. Many of the struggles were the result of poor choices that had grim consequences. In the panic and chaos of these moments, it was difficult to find the answer for "the why" bad things happen to good people.

Success stories and good outcomes did occur. Sometimes it was just not easy to have compassion, especially when human nature turned ugly. However, I always tried to achieve the best outcome for my patient. It was my job.

I may not have had a hermit who entered my life and handed me a three-legged stool, but I like to think that somehow now, sitting on these red bricks, that I managed to end up at the same place where he would have led me. Somehow, I learned that it was always about the GIVING!

Also, it is about selflessness. It is about a three-legged stool and finding of deeper kind of love. Somehow, even without a hermit I became aware of the kind of love that makes you take action. A kind of love that is hard to abandon. It is sacrificial love for another person, that love that is supposed to be between a husband and a wife. It is the love that overlooks misgivings and never doubts.

Even with all this awareness I continue to wrestle with a true understanding of selflessness and complete surrender. But, I'd like to think that I'm getting closer. I wish that I had a man such as the hermit here with me now to show me the way.

May you stop and ponder this final thought:

You may not be a secretary in a position of authority, but you can choose to give someone a cookie. You may never be in a situation of complete helplessness, but you can choose to hold someone's hand when they are moments away from dying. It is all about the giving, the giving of the self, even to the point of complete surrender.

Made in the USA
Middletown, DE
05 November 2020

23369341R00135